The Least You Should Know About English

The Least You Should Know About English

Basic Writing Skills

TERESA FERSTER GLAZIER
Western Illinois University

HOLT, RINEHART AND WINSTON
New York   Chicago   San Francisco   Atlanta
Dallas   Montreal   Toronto

Library of Congress Cataloging in Publication Data

Glazier, Teresa Ferster.
    The least you should know about English.
    1.   English language—Composition and exercises.
I.   Title.
PE1413.G57   808'.042   76-44424
ISBN: 0-03-018131-3

To the Instructor

This book is for students who have resisted the rules of English composition for twelve years and who may profit from a simplified approach.

1. It's basic. Only the indisputable essentials of spelling, grammar, sentence structure, and punctuation are included because experience has shown that teaching a lot of such things is not the best way to help students write.

2. It's simple. Most grammar terms are avoided. Gerund, past participle, indirect object, relative pronoun . . . are never mentioned. A conjunction is *a connecting word,* an antecedent is *the word referred to,* and a parenthetical expression is *an interrupter.* The students work with words they know rather than having to learn an extensive vocabulary they'll never use again.

3. It's concise. It doesn't overwhelm students with pages of inductive explanations. It simply gives them a rule and lets them learn it by using it in sentences. And it doesn't make them read pages of exposition *about* writing; it lets them begin writing at once.

4. It has plenty of practice sentences—one hundred for each rule.

5. It has perforated answer sheets in the back of the book so that the students can check their progress as they work.

6. It involves the students. Besides doing the practice exercises, they make up sentences of their own.

7. It takes modern usage into account. Accepted forms (as reported by Robert G. Pooley in *The Teaching of English Usage*) such as *It is me* and *Everybody . . . they* are recognized.

8. It emphasizes writing. Simple writing assignments, grouped together in the back of the book for convenience, are used along with the exercises. Progressing from free writing and personal writing to persuasive writing with a thesis statement, they help students discover that writing can be satisfying and enjoyable. Finally, the book includes the one kind of writing most likely to be used after college—the letter of application.

9. It includes, for the benefit of the instructor, ditto master tests *ready to run,* covering each section of the book. They are available free upon adoption of the text. Or, you may write to English Editor, Holt, Rinehart, Winston, 383 Madison Avenue, New York, New York, 10017.

Students who have heretofore been overwhelmed and discouraged by the complexities of English should, through mastering simple rules and through writing and rewriting simple compositions, gain enough confidence to cope with a regular composition course.

T.F.G.
Macomb, Illinois
November 1976

Contents

The Least You Should Know About English

What Is the Least You Should Know?

1 What **Is** the Least You Should Know?

Most English workbooks try to teach you as much as they can. This one will teach you the least it can—and still help you get by in college English courses. You won't have to bother with predicate nouns and subordinating conjunctions and participial phrases and demonstrative pronouns and all those terms you have been hearing about for years. You can get along without them if you will learn thoroughly a few basic rules. You *do* have to know how to spell common words; you *do* have to recognize subjects and verbs to avoid writing fragments and run-together sentences; you *do* have to know a few rules of punctuation—but rules will be kept to a minimum.

Unless you know these few rules, though, you will have difficulty communicating in writing. Take this sentence for example:

Let's eat grandfather before we go.

We assume the writer is not a cannibal but that he merely failed to capitalize and put commas around the name of a person spoken to. If he had written

Let's eat, Grandfather, before we go.

then no one would misunderstand. Or take this sentence:

The instructor flunked Mac and Chris and Ken passed.

Did Chris flunk or pass? There's no way of knowing unless the writer puts a comma either after *Mac* or after *Chris*. If he writes

The instructor flunked Mac and Chris, and Ken passed.

we know Chris flunked, but if he writes

The instructor flunked Mac, and Chris and Ken passed.

then we know Chris passed. What you will learn in this course is simply

2

a few rules to help make your writing so clear that no one will misunderstand it.

The English you will learn to write in this course is called Standard English, and it may be slightly different from the English spoken in your community. All over the United States, various dialects of English are spoken. In northern New England, for example, people leave the *r* off certain words and put an *r* on others. Former President Kennedy used to say *dollah* for *dollar, idear* for *idea,* and *Cubar* for *Cuba.* In black communities many people leave the *s* off some verbs and put an *s* on others, saying *he walk* and *they walks* instead of *he walks* and *they walk.*

But no matter what English dialect people *speak,* they all must write the same dialect—Standard English. You can say, "Whacha doin? Cmon," and everybody will understand you, but you can't write that way. If you want your readers to understand what you write without having to decipher it like a foreign language, you will have to write the way English-speaking people all over the world write—in Standard English. Being able to write Standard English is essential in college, and it probably will be an asset in your career.

Learning to write is like learning math. You can get along in life without algebra and geometry, but you can't get along very well without simple addition and subtraction. So it is with writing. You can get along without many of the complicated rules, but you can't get along without a few simple ones. Most of us would rather buckle down and memorize the addition and subtraction tables than count on our fingers and toes the rest of our lives. Likewise it makes sense to learn a few rules of writing now rather than to muddle along never knowing how to write properly.

It is important that you learn every rule as you come to it because many rules depend on the ones before. For example, unless you learn to pick out subjects and verbs, you will have trouble with run-together sentences, with fragments, with subject-verb agreement, and with punctuation. The rules in this workbook are brief and clear, and it should not be difficult to master all of them . . . **if you want to.** But you do have to want to!

Here is the way to master **the least you should know:**

1. Do the first exercise (ten sentences) and correct your answers by using the perforated answer sheet in the back of the book. If you miss even one answer, study the entire explanatory page again to find out why.
2. Do the second exercise and correct it. If you miss a single answer, go back once more and study the explanatory page. You must have

missed something. Be tough on yourself. Don't just think, "Maybe I'll hit it right next time." Go back and master the rules, and *then* try the next exercise. It is important to correct each group of ten sentences before going on. That way you will discover your mistakes while you still have sentences to practice on.

3. You may be tempted to quit when you get several exercises perfect, but don't do it. Make yourself finish every single exercise. It's not enough to *understand* a rule; you have to practice it. Just as understanding passing and shooting in basketball won't help unless you actually get out there onto the court and play, so understanding a rule about writing isn't going to help unless you practice using it until it becomes automatic. That's why hundreds of practice sentences have been put in this workbook.

But rules and exercises are not the most important part of this book. The most important part begins on page 190—when you begin to write. The writing assignments, grouped together for convenience, are to be used along with the exercises. Writing is the fun part of English. We all have ideas we'd like to express, and the writing assignments will help you get started. Don't be discouraged if your first writing isn't great. You learn to write by writing, and the more you write the better your writing will be.

Mastering these essentials will take time. Generally, college students are expected to spend two hours outside of class for each hour in class. You will need at least a half hour for the exercises and at least an hour and a half for the writing assignments. You may need more. Undoubtedly, the more time you spend, the more your writing will improve.

2

Spelling

2   Spelling

Anyone can learn to spell. You can get rid of most of your spelling errors by the time you finish this workbook **if you want to.** Simply follow the five suggestions given in this section.

SUGGESTION I. On page 291 in the back of this book write correctly every misspelled word in the papers handed back to you. Review them every day until you have them memorized. That will take care of most of your errors. As a starter for your list, write these two expressions that you possibly misspell:

> all right
> a lot

Take a good look at them, copy them onto page 291, and from now on remember that each of them is two words.

SUGGESTION II. Learn some words in pairs and try to find memory aids to help you remember them.

WORDS OFTEN CONFUSED

a, an	Use *an* before a word that begins with a vowel sound (*a, e, i, o, u*).
	    an orange, an essay, an heir (silent *h*), an honest man (silent *h*), an understanding.
	Use *a* before a word that begins with a consonant sound (all the other sounds except the vowels).
	    a pencil, a hotel, a history book, a university (here the *u* sound is really a consonant sound like yū instead of like the vowel sound of *u* in *understanding* above).

accept, except	*Accept* is a verb. (Verbs are explained on p. 36.) Use *except* when it's not a verb.

I *accept* your invitation.
Everyone came *except* him.
Note: *Except* can occasionally be a verb, but you are not likely to need that usage.

advice, advise

Advise is a verb. Use *advice* when it's not a verb.
Do you *advise* me to go?
I don't need *advice*.

affect, effect

Affect is a verb. Use *effect* when it's not a verb.
The lack of rain *affected* the crops.
The lack of rain had an *effect* on the crops.
Note: *Effect* can occasionally be a verb, but you are not likely to need that usage.

all ready, already

If you can leave out the *all* and the sentence still makes sense, then *all ready* is the form to use.
We are *all ready* to go. (*We are ready to go* makes sense.)
Dinner is *all ready*. (*Dinner is ready* makes sense.)
If you can't leave out the *all* and still have the sentence make sense, then use *already* (the one that has the *all* left in it).
We are *already* late. (*We are ready late* does not make sense.)

choose, chose

I *choose* a partner today.
I *chose* a partner yesterday.

clothes, cloths

Her *clothes* were not expensive.
We used soft *cloths* to polish the car.

coarse, course

Her dress is made of *coarse* cloth.
English is an easy *course*.
Of *course* I'll go.

complement, compliment

Compliment means "praise." Remember "I like compliments," and you will remember to use the *i* spelling. The spelling with *e* means "something that completes."
She gave him a *compliment*.
A thirty-degree angle is the *complement* of a sixty-degree angle.

conscience, conscious

My *conscience* bothers me because I ignored him.
I was not *conscious* that it was raining.

desert, dessert

Dessert is the sweet one, the one you like two helpings of. So give it two helpings of *s*. The other one, *desert*, is used for all other meanings.

We had apple pie for *dessert*.
Don't *desert* me.
The camel moved slowly across the *desert*.

does, dose | *Does* is a verb. A *dose* is an amount of medicine.
He *does* his work well.
She *doesn't* care about cars.
He took a *dose* of medicine.

forth, fourth | *Fourth* with *four* in it is a number. Otherwise use *forth*.
This is our *fourth* game.
She walked back and *forth*.

its, it's | *Its* is a possessive (see p. 27). *It's* always means "it is" or "it has."
The committee gave *its* report.
It's too late now.
It's been a long time.

lead, led | *Lead* is pronounced *lēēd*.
I *lead* the parade today.
I am going to *lead* the parade tomorrow.
I will *lead* the parade tomorrow.
I *led* the parade yesterday.

loose, lose | My shoelace is *l o o s e*.
Note how l o o s e that word is. It has plenty of room for two *o*'s. The other one, *lose*, has room for only one *o*.
I hope I don't *lose* my car keys.

moral, morale | Pronounce these two words correctly, and you won't confuse them—móral, morále.
It was a *moral* question.
The *morale* of the team was excellent.

passed, past | *Passed* is a verb. Use *past* when it's not a verb.
He *passed* the course.
He *passed* the detour without noticing it.
He drove right *past* the detour without noticing it.
He is living in the *past*.
He was going on his *past* reputation.

peace, piece | Remember "piece of pie." The one meaning "a *piece* of something" always begins with *pie*. The other one, *peace*, is the opposite of war.
I gave him a *piece* of my mind.
They signed the *peace* treaty.

personal, personnel | Pronounce these two correctly, and you won't confuse them—pérsonal, personnél.

He had a *personal* interest in the election.
He was in charge of *personnel* in the factory.

principal, principle	*Principal* means "main." Both words have *a* in them: principal main The *principal* of the school spoke. (main teacher) The *principal* difficulty is time. (main difficulty) He lost both *principal* and interest. (main amount of money) A *principle* is a "rule." Both words end in *le*: principle rule He lived by his *principles*. (rules) I object to the *principle* of the thing. (rule)
quiet, quite	Pronounce these two correctly, and you won't misspell them. *Quiet* is pronounced *qui et*. Be *quiet*. The book is *quite* interesting.
than, then	*Than* compares things. *Then* refers to time. (It sounds like *when*.) I'd rather have this *than* that. *Then* he started home.
their, they're, there	*Their* is a possessive (see p. 27). *They're* always means "they are." *There* points out something. *Their* only hope lay in punting. *They're* planning to come. *There* is where I left it. *There* were clouds in the sky.
to, too, two	*Two* is a number. *Too* means "more than enough" or "also." Use *to* for all other meanings. I have *two* brothers. The lesson was *too* difficult and *too* long. (more than enough) I found it difficult *too*. (also) It was *too* much for *two* people *to* eat.
weather, whether	*Weather* refers to atmospheric conditions. *Whether* means "if." *Whether* I'll go depends on the *weather*.
whose, who's	*Whose* is a possessive (see p. 27). *Who's* always means "who is" or "who has." *Whose* book is this? *Who's* there? *Who's* been using my tennis racket?

your, you're   *Your* is a possessive (see p. 27). *You're* always means "you are."
          Your toast is ready.
          You're very welcome.

EXERCISES

Underline the correct word. Don't guess! Refer to the explanatory pages if necessary. When you have finished ten sentences, tear out the perforated answer sheet in the back of the book and correct your answers. Correct **each ten** before going on. Answers to the exercises start on page 213.

☐EXERCISE 1

1. We are not (quiet quite) ready for (desert dessert).
2. (There They're) going to (accept except) the invitation.
3. (Who's Whose) idea was it to sign up for that (coarse course)?
4. He (lead led) the procession (passed past) the courthouse.
5. My father's (advice advise) had no (affect effect) on me.
6. Everyone wants (peace piece) and (quiet quite).
7. I had (all ready already) bought my (clothes cloths) for the trip.
8. (Does Dose) he mind the hot (weather whether)?
9. I should heed my (conscience conscious).
10. I'm at (loose lose) ends and just about ready to (loose lose) my mind.

☐EXERCISE 2

1. I don't know (weather whether) I (passed past) the (coarse course) or not.
2. (Your You're) not (all ready already) to go, are you?
3. (Their There) were (to too) many people in (their there) house.
4. The (affect effect) of his (advice advise) was greater (than then) he expected.
5. (Whose Who's) (principals principles) are you going to live by?
6. She received many (complements compliments) on her new (clothes cloths).
7. You never can be (quiet quite) sure of the (weather whether) in this country.
8. (Your You're) never (quiet quite) unless (your you're) asleep.
9. It (does dose) not matter if the sails are a little (loose lose).
10. (Their They're) selfishness doesn't (affect effect) me.

☐EXERCISE 3

1. I'm taking (a an) honors (coarse course) and hope to get (a an) university degree.

2. We were served (quiet quite) a good dinner (accept except) for the (desert dessert).
3. (It's Its) my (forth fourth) year in college, and I (all ready already) have next year's plans made.
4. He walked back and (forth fourth) trying to (choose chose) the right strategy.
5. I was (to too) tired and (to too) hungry to pay any attention to the (weather whether).
6. The (moral morale) in the company was so low that the (personal personnel) department had difficulty getting new workers.
7. She has learned to (accept except) (complements compliments) gracefully.
8. I don't think (their there) actions are exactly (moral morale).
9. Would you (advice advise) me to (accept except) the position?
10. (Your You're) apt to (loose lose) your chance if you don't (accept except) immediately.

□EXERCISE 4

1. It was a bitter (does dose) of medicine.
2. The captain (lead led) the team to (it's its) victory.
3. I don't know (quiet quite) what to think of his (advice advise).
4. The tramp walked back and (forth fourth) in front of the house.
5. The dog (lead led) (it's its) puppies out of the barn.
6. He gave me (a an) ugly look as he walked (passed past) me.
7. (It's Its) hard to think of (a an) answer.
8. She was (conscience conscious) of her poor (clothes cloths).
9. A (peace piece) of (loose lose) gravel hit the windshield.
10. A shack covered with (coarse course) palm leaves stood on the (desert dessert).

□EXERCISE 5

1. (Your You're) (conscience conscious) will give you the best (advice advise).
2. (It's Its) true that he has no (principals principles) to live by.
3. (Their They're) completely without (moral morale) standards.
4. With a (loose lose) scarf tied around her head, she (lead led) the way.
5. The (personal personnel) are not allowed to invest (their there) money in the firm.
6. The (principal principle) of the school spoke to him as they (passed past) each other in the hall.
7. The lecture was (quiet quite) interesting but much (to too) long (to too) suit me.

8. He will (lead led) the children to (their they're) room.
9. Yesterday he had (lead led) them out to the playground and (than then) back again.
10. He gave me a (peace piece) of (advice advise).

□EXERCISE 6

1. (Who's Whose) speech did you like best?
2. The new ruling has (affected effected) the (moral morale) of the (personal personnel) in the office.
3. The (moral morale) of the team had never been higher.
4. (Does Dose) the coach think (their there they're) prepared for the trip?
5. The team is (all ready already) to go.
6. Which (peace piece) of cloth do you like—the (coarse course) one or the fine one?
7. The gloomy house had (a an) (affect effect) on his mood.
8. (It's Its) wise to (choose chose) your (coarses courses) carefully.
9. The dean's (advice advise) had more (affect effect) on him (than then) his father's.
10. I don't know (weather whether) the (weather whether) will keep him from coming.

□EXERCISE 7

1. My (principal principle) objection to the speaker was that he paid himself (to too two) many (complements compliments).
2. (Who's Whose) (advice advise) was it in the first place?
3. (You're Your) not going to wear formal (clothes cloths), are you?
4. They (accepted excepted) the invitation to visit the pottery.
5. A child should be allowed to (choose chose) his own (clothes cloths).
6. We were served (a an) appetizer to begin the meal and a (desert dessert) to end it.
7. The children were (quiet quite) upset over the change in the (weather whether).
8. I suppose (you're your) (to too two) busy to do any reading.
9. I don't think (their there they're) plans are any better (than then) ours.
10. If I have a choice I always (choose chose) steak rather (than then) fish.

□EXERCISE 8

1. (You're Your) (advice advise) has (all ready already) been followed.
2. I had never talked to (a an) Indian before.
3. The (forth fourth) time I won.
4. Long ago he (choose chose) to follow the (moral morale) standards of his parents.

5. They looked out of (their there they're) window (passed past) the garden, which was (all ready already) in full bloom.
6. How is (you're your) (coarse course) in history?
7. (Does Dose) he give you many (complements compliments)?
8. (Their There They're) expecting a larger crowd (than then) they had last year.
9. The (weather whether) is (to too two) cold (to too) suit me.
10. The Sahara (Desert Dessert) in North Africa is the largest (desert dessert) in the world.

□EXERCISE 9

1. They marched (forth fourth) in the cause of (peace piece).
2. Mother (passed past) the (desert dessert) around the (forth fourth) time.
3. We won't (loose lose) more (than then) five dollars.
4. It was (all ready already) (passed past) midnight.
5. He (lead led) the way (passed past) the sawmill to the lake.
6. Are you (all ready already) to (choose chose) your partner?
7. (Does Dose) she eat (to too two) many chocolate bars?
8. Is that (you're your) (personal personnel) opinion?
9. She'd rather sew (than then) eat.
10. She has (all ready already) made (to too two) suits.

□EXERCISE 10

1. (Who's Whose) planning to go bowling tonight?
2. First we walked (passed past) the dam; (than then) we circled the lake.
3. It (does dose) not matter (weather whether) (you're your) on time.
4. He (choose chose) to (desert dessert) his army post that summer.
5. My (conscience conscious) wouldn't let me charge any (personal personnel) expenses to my expense account.
6. (Who's Whose) been using my car while I've been away?
7. (It's Its) not (to too two) clear (who's whose) to blame.
8. My (principal principle) difficulty (does dose) seem to be spelling.
9. Since taking this (coarse course), I spell better (than then) before.
10. I (all ready already) have a long list of words to learn.

WRITING YOUR OWN SENTENCES

Writing your own sentences is the best way to master the materials you have been studying. On a separate sheet write ten sentences using some of the words you have had trouble with.

SUGGESTION III. Learn to break words into their parts. These words are made up of two shorter words:

over run	overrun	room mate	roommate
over rate	overrate	with hold	withhold

And learn to spell such prefixes as *dis, inter, mis,* and *un.* Then when you add a word to the prefix, the spelling will be correct:

dis appear	disappear	mis spell	misspell
dis appoint	disappoint	mis step	misstep
dis approve	disapprove	un natural	unnatural
dis satisfied	dissatisfied	un necessary	unnecessary
dis service	disservice	un nerve	unnerve
inter racial	interracial	un noticed	unnoticed
inter related	interrelated		

SUGGESTION IV. Learn one spelling rule. Most spelling rules have so many exceptions that they are not much help, but here is one that has almost no exceptions and is really worth learning.

RULE FOR DOUBLING A FINAL CONSONANT

Double a final consonant when adding an ending beginning with a vowel (such as ing, ed, er) if the word

1. **ends in a single consonant,**
2. **preceded by a single vowel (the vowels are a, e, i, o, u),**
3. **and the accent is on the last syllable.**

We'll try the rule on a few words to which we'll add *ing, ed,* or *er.*

begin   1. It ends in a single consonant—*n,*
2. preceded by a single vowel—*i,*
3. and the accent is on the last syllable—*begín.*
Therefore we double the final consonant and write *beginning, beginner.*

stop   1. It ends in a single consonant—*p,*
2. preceded by a single vowel—*o,*
3. and the accent is on the last syllable (there is only one).
Therefore we double the final consonant and write *stopping, stopped, stopper.*

benefit   1. It ends in a single consonant—*t,*
2. preceded by a single vowel—*i,*
3. but the accent is not on the last syllable; it is on the first—*bénefit.*
Therefore we do not double the final consonant. We write *benefiting, benefited.*

sleep   1. It ends in a single consonant—*p,*
2. but it is not preceded by a single vowel; there are two *e's.*
Therefore we do not double the final consonant. We write *sleeping, sleeper.*

kick   1. It does not end in a single consonant. There are two—*c* and *k.*
Therefore we do not double the final consonant. We write *kicking, kicked.*

Note that *qu* is really a consonant because q is never written without *u.* (Look in your dictionary and see.) Think of it as *kw.* In words like *equip* and *quit,* the *qu* acts as a consonant. Therefore *quit* does end in a single consonant preceded by a single vowel, and the final consonant is doubled—*quitting.*

You'll be wise to skip the rest of this explanation. It concerns exceptions that you'll never have trouble with, and they may simply confuse you. They are included here merely to make the rule complete. So *skip on to the exercises.*

1. Consider *w* or *y* at the end of a word a vowel. *Row, sew, sow, toy* all end in vowels, and the rule does not apply.
2. Consider *x* at the end of a word as two consonants *ks. Box, flex, fix* all end in double consonants, and the rule does not apply.
3. One common word *bus* may be written either *bussing* or *busing.* Newspapers lately use the latter more often. Either is correct.

EXERCISES

Add **ing** to these words. Correct each group of ten by using the perforated answer sheet in the back of the book before going on.

☐EXERCISE 1

1. putting
2. controlling
3. sweeping
4. mopping
5. turning

6. hopping
7. jumping
8. knitting
9. marking
10. creeping

☐EXERCISE 2

1. returning
2. swimming
3. singing
4. benefiting
5. loafing

6. nailling
7. omitting
8. occurring
9. shopping
10. interrupting

☐EXERCISE 3

1. beginning
2. spelling
3. preferring
4. fishing
5. hunting

6. excelling
7. wrapping
8. stopping
9. wedding
10. screaming

☐EXERCISE 4

1. feelling
2. motoring

3. turning
4. adding

5. subtract*ing*
6. stream*ing*
7. expel*ling*

8. miss*ing*
9. get*ting*
10. stress*ing*

☐**EXERCISE 5**

1. forget*ting*
2. misspell*ing*
3. fit*ting*
4. plant*ing*
5. pin*ning*

6. trust*ing*
7. sip*ping*
8. flop*ping*
9. reap*ing*
10. cart*ing*

☐**EXERCISE 6**

1. attend*ing*
2. compel*ling*
3. nap*ping*
4. curl*ling*
5. amount*ing*

6. obtain*hing*
7. dream*ing*
8. crawl*ing*
9. crop*ping*
10. descend*ing*

☐**EXERCISE 7**

1. permit*ting*
2. despair*ing*
3. eat*ing*
4. develop*ing*
5. quit*ting*

6. exceed*ing*
7. finish*ing*
8. hit*ting*
9. flinch*ing*
10. refer*ring*

☐**EXERCISE 8**

1. regard*ing*
2. equip*ing*
3. kick*ing*
4. sit*ting*
5. knock*ing*

6. sleep*ing*
7. skip*ping*
8. leap*ing*
9. ship*ping*
10. mention*ing*

☐**EXERCISE 9**

1. stir*ring*
2. mend*ing*
3. shriek*ing*
4. murmur*ing*
5. view*ing*

6. meet*ing*
7. speak*ing*
8. succeed*ing*
9. pretend*ing*
10. defer*ring*

□EXERCISE 10

1. pull*ing*
2. predict*ing*
3. redeem*ing*
4. patroll*ing*
5. slant*ing*

6. steam*ing*
7. rip*ping*
8. spend*ing*
9. tip*ping*
10. trip*ping*

SUGGESTION V. Have someone dictate this list of commonly misspelled words and mark those you miss. Memorize the words you miss and any you are not sure of from previous pages. Once a week have someone dictate to you words from these lists and from the list you are keeping in the back of the book.

SPELLING LIST

1. absence	38. description	75. interest
2. accept	39. desperate	76. interfere
3. across	40. development	77. involved
4. address	41. difference	78. judgment
5. adviser	42. different	79. knowledge
6. almost	43. discipline	80. laboratory
7. already	44. discussed	81. learned
8. although	45. divide	82. leisure
9. always	46. eighth	83. length
10. among	47. eligible	84. library
11. amount	48. eliminate	85. license
12. answer	49. embarrassed	86. likely
13. athlete	50. escape	87. marriage
14. athletics	51. etc.	88. mathematics
15. becoming	52. exaggerate	89. meant
16. beginning	53. excellent	90. necessary
17. belief	54. experience	91. neither
18. believe	55. explain	92. ninety
19. buried	56. explanation	93. ninth
20. business	57. extremely	94. occasionally
21. careful	58. familiar	95. occur
22. certain	59. finally	96. occurred
23. college	60. foreign	97. opinion
24. coming	61. forty	98. opportunity
25. committee	62. friend	99. paid
26. competition	63. government	100. particular
27. consider	64. grateful	101. perform
28. control	65. guarantee	102. performance
29. counselor	66. guidance	103. planned
30. criticism	67. height	104. possess
31. criticize	68. (it) helped	105. possible
32. decision	69. hoping	106. practical
33. definite	70. humorous	107. preferred
34. definitely	71. immediately	108. prejudice
35. definition	72. independence	109. preparation
36. dependent	73. independent	110. pressure
37. describe	74. intelligence	111. privilege

112. probably
113. procedure
114. proceed
115. professor
116. proof
117. prove
118. pursue
119. realize
120. receipt
121. receive
122. recommend
123. relieve
124. religious
125. repetition
126. rhythm
127. ridiculous
128. sacrifice
129. safety
130. scene
131. schedule
132. science
133. seize
134. separate
135. several
136. severe
137. shining
138. significant
139. similar
140. sophomore
141. speech
142. straight
143. studying
144. succeed
145. supposed (to)
146. surprise
147. temperature
148. together
149. tragedy
150. tried
151. truly
152. until
153. unusual
154. used (to)
155. using
156. usually
157. Wednesday
158. (one) woman
159. (two) women
160. writing

CONTRACTIONS

Two words condensed into one are called a contraction.

is not	isn't
you have	you've

The letter or letters that are left out are replaced with an apostrophe. For example, if the two words *do not* are condensed into one, an apostrophe is put where the *o* is left out.

do not	don't

Note how the apostrophe goes in the exact place where the letter or letters are left out in these contractions:

I am	I'm
you are	you're
he is	he's
we are	we're
they are	they're
there is	there's
it is	it's
it has	it's
he has	he's
they have	they've
I shall	I'll
she will	she'll
I would	I'd
they would	they'd
are not	aren't
cannot	can't
do not	don't
have not	haven't
should not	shouldn't
let us	let's
who is	who's
who has	who's
where is	where's

One contraction does not follow this rule:

will not	won't

In all other contractions that you are likely to use, the apostrophe goes exactly where the letter or letters have been left out.

Note especially *it's, they're, who's,* and *you're.* Use them whenever you mean two words. See page 27 for the possessive forms—*its, their, whose,* and *your.*

EXERCISES

Put an apostrophe where a letter or letters have been left out. In the first sentence for example, you will put an apostrophe in **Let's.** Tear out the perforated answer sheet in the back of the book, and correct each group of ten sentences before going on.

□EXERCISE 1

1. Lets go to the City Council meeting.
2. Doesnt the spring weather make you feel lazy?
3. Arent you coming to the game?
4. I dont like the climate here; its too cold.
5. Were studying World War II in history now.
6. Im in the swimming club this year.
7. Doesnt he care which candidate wins?
8. I cant see why hes so obstinate.
9. Dont you have any afternoon classes?
10. Youve been absent for a long time, havent you?

□EXERCISE 2

1. Its all right for you to leave.
2. The cat drank its milk from the saucer.
3. I dont think Ill vote for that amendment.
4. Whos running for president of the club?
5. He doesnt approve of the gun lobby.
6. The proposed law doesnt have enough support to carry it.
7. The dog buried its bone in the backyard.
8. Its too bad hes not coming.
9. Youre planning to travel this summer, arent you?
10. One cant skate on dull skates.

□EXERCISE 3

1. Youll return these chairs soon, wont you?
2. Dont forget Im leaving for Chicago next week.
3. I cant imagine why hes late.
4. Arent you going to play tennis?

5. It isn't as if we weren't sorry.
6. I shouldn't eat this, and I wouldn't if it didn't taste so good.
7. It's wings were black and it's tail feathers gray.
8. I can't say a thing that she doesn't disagree with.
9. I couldn't have worked harder if I'd been paid.
10. That's the little man who wasn't there.

□EXERCISE 4

1. I won't be gone long. Won't you come too?
2. Of course we're expecting to win. Why shouldn't we?
3. Can't we be friends?
4. I wouldn't have missed you if you hadn't taken the car.
5. Don't you ever study?
6. I'll not be surprised if a dark horse wins.
7. My puppy had it's first trip to the vet today.
8. What's going to happen if he doesn't show up?
9. That's the way it's always been.
10. Don't you want to go?

□EXERCISE 5

1. Hes been to Europe, but he hasnt been west of New York.
2. Im sorry you couldnt come.
3. Dont ever think you can fool him.
4. Im reading one old book now for every new one I read.
5. Im always making budgets and never following them.
6. Ive been working hard but still havent finished.
7. Havent you heard the meadowlarks? Theyve been here for weeks.
8. I think Im going to Florida next week, but Im not sure.
9. Do as you like, but dont say I failed to warn you.
10. I cant figure out why I didnt hear the alarm.

□EXERCISE 6

1. Im in favor of a new system of spelling—my system.
2. Youd be tired too if youd studied as late as I did.
3. Lets listen to the Elton John album tonight.
4. Cant you come?
5. Thats too bad.
6. Wont you sit down?
7. Hows your disposition this morning?
8. Dont worry about me.

9. Im all right now; Ive finished my assignment.
10. Its fortunate that shes even-tempered.

□EXERCISE 7

1. Its true that rewriting teaches one to write.
2. Its fun to be in the choral group even if you cant sing.
3. College would be fun if one didnt have to go to classes.
4. Cant you come if I wait until four?
5. He couldnt explain the problem because he didnt understand it.
6. Were going rowing this afternoon if it isnt too cold.
7. That isnt true, and it isnt fair.
8. Id like to be at the lake right now.
9. Wed made our preparations and then couldnt go.
10. The speaker didnt arrive until nine.

□EXERCISE 8

1. Its not as if we werent prepared.
2. Ive never heard such nonsense.
3. I dont know what were supposed to do.
4. Yes, Ill go, but its not because I want to.
5. Im afraid youre too late now.
6. Id rather be a big duck in a little pond than a little duck in a big pond.
7. Twos company; threes a crowd.
8. Whos your partner?
9. I wouldnt mind working if I didnt have to hurry.
10. Hes the most generous person Ive ever known.

□EXERCISE 9

1. Youre more conscientious than shes ever been.
2. Thats all Ive heard about it.
3. Isnt that just like her to say shes too busy?
4. Dont be afraid to try your wings.
5. He never gets much done because he hasnt learned to say no.
6. Weve postponed the trip until shes able to go.
7. Shes learned to study no matter whos in the room.
8. It isnt difficult to increase your vocabulary if youre interested in words.
9. Youll never learn to punctuate sentences until youve learned to pick out subjects and verbs.
10. Theyre in no condition for a game.

□EXERCISE 10

1. Shes a perfect hostess.

2. Theyd gone almost all the way to the auditorium when they realized they hadnt brought their tickets.
3. Ive decided Ill learn to spell if it kills me.
4. Wasnt the stage setting effective, and werent the costumes beautiful?
5. Im trying to educate my parents, but its a difficult job.
6. Were likely to spend too much time assimilating and not enough creating.
7. There isnt anyone who doesnt get a thrill out of creating, even if its nothing more than a fancy birthday cake.
8. Theres no more delightful climate in summer than that of the Green Mountains in Vermont.
9. Its necessary to have a dictionary in this course.
10. My mother isnt happy unless shes digging in the garden.

WRITING YOUR OWN SENTENCES

On a separate sheet write five sentences using contractions, especially any you have had trouble with.

POSSESSIVES

The trick in writing possessives is to ask yourself the question, "Who does it belong to?" (Modern usage has made *who* acceptable when it comes first in a sentence, but if you want to sound like an old-fashioned English teacher, you can say, "*Whom* does it belong to?" or even "*To whom* does it belong?") If the answer to your question does not end in *s*, then add an apostrophe and *s*. If it does end in *s*, simply add an apostrophe.

one boys bike	Who does it belong to?	boy	Add *'s*	the boy's bike
two boys bikes	Who do they belong to?	boys	Add *'*	the boys' bikes
the mans hat	Who does it belong to?	man	Add *'s*	the man's hat
the mens hats	Who do they belong to?	men	Add *'s*	the men's hats
childrens game	Who does it belong to?	children	Add *'s*	children's game
one girls coat	Who does it belong to?	girl	Add *'s*	girl's coat
two girls coats	Who do they belong to?	girls	Add *'*	girls' coats

This trick will always work, but you must remember to ask the question each time. If you just look at the word, you may think the name of the owner ends in an *s* when it really doesn't.

Cover the right-hand column and see if you can write the following possessives correctly. Ask the question each time.

the womans dress	woman's
the womens ideas	women's
Jacks apartment	Jack's
James apartment	James'
the Smiths house	the Smiths'
Mr. Smiths house	Mr. Smith's

(Sometime you may see a variation of this rule. *James' book* may be written *James's book*. That is correct too, but the best way is to stick to the simple rule given above. You can't be wrong if you follow it.)

In such expressions as *a day's work* or *Saturday's game,* you may ask how the work can belong to the day or the game can belong to Saturday. Those are simply possessive forms that have been in our language for a long time. And when you think about it, the work really does belong to the day (not the night), and the game does belong to Saturday (not Friday).

A word of warning! Don't assume that because a word ends in *s* it is necessarily a possessive. Make sure the word actually possesses something before you put in an apostrophe.

Possessive pronouns are already possessive and don't need anything added to them.

my, mine	its
your, yours	our, ours
his	their, theirs
her, hers	whose

Note particularly *its, their, whose,* and *your.* They do not take apostrophes (see p. 21 for the contractions, the forms that stand for two words and take apostrophes). As a review, cover the right-hand column below, and write the correct form (contraction or possessive) in the blank. Then check your answers. If you miss any, go back and review the instructions on contractions and possessives.

(It) raining.	It's
(You) car needs washing.	Your
(Who) to blame?	Who's
(They) planning to come.	They're
The cat drank (it) milk.	its
(Who) been sitting here?	Who's
The wind lost (it) force.	its
(Who) going with me?	Who's
My book has lost (it) cover.	its
(It) all I can do.	It's
(You) right.	You're
(They) garden has many trees.	Their
(It) sunny today.	It's
(Who) car shall we take?	Whose
The club lost (it) leader.	its
(Who) umbrella is that?	Whose
(You) too late now.	You're
I have lost (they) address.	their
Do you have (you) ticket?	your
(They) always late.	They're

EXERCISES

Put the apostrophe in each possessive. Don't be confused because there is already an **s** on the possessive. Ask the question "Who does it belong to?" and then you will know where to put the apostrophe. In the first sentence, for example, "Who did the watch belong to?" "Girl." Therefore you will write **girl's.** And make sure the word really does possess something before you put in an apostrophe. Correct each exercise before going on.

□EXERCISE 1

1. I saw a girls watch on the table.
2. They slept in the lone mountain rangers cabin.
3. Have you seen Neds new Cougar and Dennis new Mustang?
4. Do you sell mens overcoats?
5. I'm going to stay at my brother-in-laws camp.
6. The track teams trophy is displayed in the entrance hall.
7. Normas mother is head of the local League of Women Voters.
8. The audiences applause was tremendous.
9. The dog stood on its hind legs.
10. He couldn't understand the teams weak line of defense.

□EXERCISE 2

1. The ladies enjoyed the chairpersons jokes.
2. I'm afraid Terrys studying is interfering with his social life.
3. We were all impressed with the senators speech.
4. Jeffreys ability in dramatics may carry him far.
5. Someones cat crawled in the window.
6. Annettes cheeks were flushed.
7. Yesterdays game was the best of the season.
8. The committee planned its publicity for the Bloodmobile.
9. They hid the photo that was on Georges study table.
10. Last nights party lasted until dawn.

□EXERCISE 3

1. Do you plan to join the Womens Club?
2. The worlds tallest known species of tree is the coast redwood.
3. Maybe I can get Dads car.
4. Have you read Haleys Roots?
5. We spent Thanksgiving at Uncle Lloyds cottage.
6. The visitors were impressed with Dads garden.
7. I don't like having to do someone elses job.
8. My brothers roommate is here for the weekend.

9. Toms watch is invariably slow.
10. Charles car was parked in the driveway.

☐EXERCISE 4

1. The girls voices were low and tense.
2. The gardens are all drying up.
3. He wasn't listening to his wifes words.
4. His fathers word was law.
5. The bird didn't abandon its nest until its young were able to fly.
6. Archibalds chief diversion is reading philosophy.
7. The Sacramento River raged against its banks.
8. A childs conduct is dependent on his parents attitude.
9. I had read all of Dickens novels by the time I was fourteen.
10. Geralds motto seems to be to study hard—the night before exams.

☐EXERCISE 5

1. Chicagos skyline isn't as impressive as New Yorks.
2. The clubs first president served four years.
3. I like Bob Dylans poems.
4. That colleges chief claim to fame is its football team.
5. It was hard to accept that judges decision.
6. Mr. Jones keeps his lawn in beautiful condition.
7. Mr. Jones lawn is in beautiful condition.
8. Have you ever seen Niagara Falls in the winter?
9. I borrowed Dianas bicycle.
10. Everyone was pleased about Nancys summer job.

☐EXERCISE 6

1. Childrens symphonies are now being organized in many cities.
2. They didn't know what to do with Harrys guitar.
3. He had left his guitar in its case at the Student Union.
4. He refused to take anybodys word on the matter.
5. The library had its annual book sale Saturday.
6. The note invited him to the deans office.
7. Each days work should give one a sense of achievement.
8. We were tired after Saturdays workout.
9. Are you going to the governors reception?
10. The car lost its grip on the road.

☐EXERCISE 7

1. The presidents veto was a surprise.

2. Jerrys desk is always in order.
3. I was surprised at Pauls courage.
4. We were all invited to the twins party.
5. The young colt was standing by its mother.
6. My dads car is smaller than my mothers.
7. We stopped to see Peters puppet theater.
8. The childs disappointment was plain.
9. We must consider the car dealers reputation too.
10. Ralphs mind isn't exactly on his studies these days.

□EXERCISE 8

1. The settlers hard work and courage helped them through the hard winter.
2. What was Babe Ruths batting average?
3. The bartenders eyes widened with astonishment.
4. Beethovens Fifth Symphony is a masterful elaboration of the "fate motif."
5. This motif was one of the French peoples secret symbols during World War II.
6. Lincolns gaunt frame was a comforting sight to the North during the Civil War.
7. The mothers eyes met her daughters.
8. His grades show his determination to get ahead.
9. The chief asset of that house is its charming garden.
10. Hurrying out of the room, he grabbed someone elses books instead of his own.

□EXERCISE 9

1. Teds motor scooter is faster than Toms.
2. Their sweaters were covered with snow.
3. As the plane descended, its wings became icy.
4. The students commencement gowns did not arrive in time.
5. Who will win the primary is anybodys guess.
6. The professor read everybodys paper in class.
7. The professors comments were interesting.
8. Someones paper had excellent specific details.
9. I've never eaten meals as good as my mothers.
10. Chaucers tales have stood the test of time.

□EXERCISE 10

1. The car in front of their house isn't theirs.
2. It's the Johnsons car.

3. My fathers hobby is collecting rock and mineral specimens.
4. Whose book is this?
5. It's probably either Marthas or Sarahs.
6. I'm not asking for anyones advice.
7. The Womens Club held its regular meeting Thursday.
8. James advice differed from Ervins.
9. Most of Michaels time is spent in studying.
10. The store sells only mens and boys clothing.

WRITING YOUR OWN SENTENCES

On a separate sheet write five sentences using possessives, especially ones you might sometime use in an essay or a letter.

Review Exercises for Contractions and Possessives

Put the apostrophes in these contractions and possessives. In trying to get all your exercises perfect, don't say, "Oh, that was just a careless mistake," and excuse it. A mistake is a mistake. Be tough on yourself.

□EXERCISE 1

1. Shes hoping shell be invited to the Faulkners party.
2. Will you mail Berts letters for him?
3. Shouldnt we go with them?
4. Wouldnt you like to join our party?
5. They invited Charles to their cabin.
6. I left my books on the doorstep, but yours are in the car.
7. Wont you give the dog its food?
8. I cant study tonight, for James didnt bring my books.
9. Weve been listening to a dry-as-dust lecture.
10. I agree with Carlyles theory of work.

□EXERCISE 2

1. Did you hear Eric Claptons live concert on the radio?
2. I imagined Id do as I pleased when I was twenty-one.
3. Thats whats bothering me.
4. Theres nothing pretentious about Harolds car.
5. Dads flower garden is his hobby.
6. Jims interest in electronics isnt just a passing phase.
7. Cant you come to Janets house for the meeting?
8. She couldnt or wouldnt give us permission to try Beckys idea.
9. Isnt it a shame shes not making use of her talents?
10. His lecture wasnt long, but it inspired us all.

□EXERCISE 3

1. Its true that Morris is going to his uncles farm to work.
2. It didnt take long to discover I had someone elses coat.
3. Yesterday afternoon we went to Hazels apartment for a snack.
4. I didnt take the clerks advice.
5. I wont be going to Saturdays game.
6. Shes proud of her mothers achievement.
7. After an hours wait I walked out.
8. Were expecting a test tomorrow.

9. Didnt you know the football season is over?
10. Im sure were on the right road.

□EXERCISE 4

1. Dont tell Douglas that its his last chance.
2. Theres to be an inspection tour of the students lockers.
3. Im not sure of Ruths address.
4. Were hoping to get a ride in Mr. Jones new van.
5. Heres your pay.
6. Dad blew up when he saw Garys grades.
7. Ive heard that Louis is leaving tomorrow.
8. Theirs was the first party of the season.
9. Dont you approve of Womens Liberation?
10. Im sure he wont approve of Vivians extravagance.

□EXERCISE 5

1. Isnt it a shame shes missing the party?
2. Shouldnt you leave a note for Francis brother?
3. Its about time for the coachs speech.
4. Is the bike yours or Mikes?
5. I wouldnt think shed want to go.
6. Its getting cold; Im going in.
7. The childrens play equipment is no longer useful; its worn out.
8. Wont you join the student debating society?
9. Whose advice are you going to take—your dads or your moms?
10. They sell both womens and mens shoes.

Sentence Structure
and Agreement

3 Sentence Structure and Agreement

The most common errors in freshman writing are fragments and run-together sentences. Here are some fragments:

Having given the best years of his life to his farm
Although we had food enough for only one day
The most that I possibly could do
Even though I tried very hard

They don't make complete statements. They leave the reader wanting something more.

Here are some run-together sentences:

We missed Nancy she is always the life of the party.
We had a wonderful time everyone was in a great mood.
I worked hard I should have got a better grade.
It was raining the pavement was slippery.

Unlike fragments, they make complete statements, but the trouble is they make *two* complete statements which should not be run together into one sentence. The reader has to go back to see where he should have paused.

Both fragments and run-together sentences bother the reader. Not until you can get rid of them will your writing be clear and easy to read. Unfortunately there is no quick, easy way to learn to avoid them. You have to learn a little about sentence structure—mainly how to find the subject and the verb in a sentence so that you can tell whether it really is a sentence.

FINDING SUBJECTS AND VERBS

When you write a sentence, you write about *something* or *someone*. That is the subject. Then you write what the subject *does* or *is*. That is the verb.

Birds fly.

The word *Birds* is the something you are writing about. It's the subject, and we'll underline it once. *Fly* tells what the subject *does*. It's the verb, and we'll underline it twice.

36

Since the verb often tells what the subject does, it is easier to spot than the subject. First spot the verb in a sentence and then ask *Who* or *What.* For example, if the verb is *fly,* ask *who* or *what* flies. The answer will be the subject. Study the following sentences until you understand how to find subjects and verbs.

Birds fly north in the spring. (Who or what flies? Birds fly.)

Migrating birds fly north in the spring and south in the fall. (Who or what flies? Birds fly.)

John drove his car. (Who or what drove? John drove.)

Last week John drove his car to the coast. (Who or what drove? John drove.)

After finishing classes John drove his car to his home on the coast. (Who or what drove? John drove.)

The following verbs don't show what the subject *does.* They show what the subject *is* or *was.*

Nick is my brother. (Who or what is? Nick is.)

That boy in the blue jeans and red shirt is my younger brother. (Who or what is? Boy is.)

That boy standing by the car with the tan top is my brother. (Who or what is? Boy is.)

Melanie seems happy these days. (Who or what seems? Melanie seems.)

The movie was interesting. (Who or what was? Movie was.)

Sometimes the subject comes after the verb.

In the stands were five thousand spectators. (Who or what were? Spectators were.)

Down the street came the procession. (Who or what came? Procession came.)

There was a large crowd at the party. (Who or what was? Crowd was.)

There were not nearly enough plates for everybody. (Who or what were? Plates were.)

Here was positive evidence. (Who or what was? Evidence was.)

Note that *there* and *here* (as in the last three sentences) are never subjects. They simply point out something.

In commands the subject often is not expressed. It is *you* (understood).

Open the door! (You open the door.)

Eat your spinach! (You eat your spinach.)

EXERCISES

Underline the subject once and the verb twice. Find the verb first, and then ask **who** or **what.** When you have done ten sentences, tear out the perforated answer sheet in the back of the book and correct your answers. Be sure to correct **each group of ten** before you go on so that you will learn from your mistakes.

□EXERCISE 1

1. The grass is green.

2. He was at the stock car races.

3. The clouds covered the mountain.

4. The newspapers exaggerated the story.

5. We sauntered among the people on the streets.

6. Slowly the crowds moved into the stadium.

7. Night comes quickly on the Sahara.

8. Your attitude is important.

9. Big cities are seldom typical of a country.

10. Higher and higher rose the flames.

□EXERCISE 2

1. Stand with the weight on the balls of your feet. *you implied*

2. During the evening heavy black clouds rolled across the sky.

3. At noon the halls are noisy.

4. The instructor stressed the importance of concentration.

5. A lizard darted from cactus to cactus.

6. There was no logical development in his paper.

7. The exhibits at the fair were educational.

8. Basketball requires a great deal of skill.

9. From an upstairs window we saw the forest fire.

10. The bed of flowers in the garden contained exotic plants.

□EXERCISE 3

1. Then came the storm.

2. The skiers wanted snowy weather.

3. At the end of the little path was a deer.

4. My younger sister at last broke the silence.

5. There was no question about her integrity.

6. Despite the undertow we swam safely to shore.

7. That book is interesting.

8. A monument to the sea gulls stands in Temple Square in Salt Lake City.

9. Man is not the only tool-using animal.

10. We found arrowheads along the river valley.

□EXERCISE 4

1. I keep a study schedule now.

2. State your major interests.

3. At noon we stopped at a village restaurant.

4. They clambered onto the wagon of hay.

5. The fire swept across the dry prairie.

6. Fortunately a motorist saw it.

7. Minutes later he alerted the fire department in the nearby town.

8. Only a small cabin on the edge of the prairie burned.

9. The country needs stricter gun control laws.

10. Jay dived off the cliff into the shallow water.

□EXERCISE 5

1. The blue jay took a drink from the birdbath.

2. Here was his chance for a touchdown.

3. Early in the morning the water rushed through the broken dikes.

4. Fear spread through the countryside.

5. The farmers made makeshift boats and rafts.

6. Still others repaired the leaking dikes.

7. Suddenly a huge wave swept over the dike and over the workers.

8. Then the sea was calm once again.

9. They were the opinions of the entire group.

10. The tapestry was machine-made.

□EXERCISE 6

1. Before long he decided against the plan.

2. Do twenty-five push-ups without stopping.

3. They went to parties every weekend.

4. There is no reason for a statement like that.

5. The shatterproof glass quivered.

6. His face looked almost gray.

7. He graduated from college at twenty-one.

8. Our group leader is a clever person.

9. He is the only serious-minded boy in the crowd.

10. The half-starved boy came slowly into camp.

□EXERCISE 7

1. The recipe calls for six eggs.

2. She received her salary on the first and the fifteenth.

3. The strikers demanded a thirty-hour week.

4. On the banks of the tiny stream were dwarf cedars.

5. The speaker is a well-known author.

6. The board included world-famous people.

7. Ted fell for the redhead.

8. We stopped at noon for a much-needed rest.

9. The people on the list reported for work yesterday.

10. Her house contained all kinds of laborsaving devices.

□EXERCISE 8

1. Hard work usually brings results.

2. One hundred million galaxies are in the bowl of the Big Dipper.

3. I have no patience with dawdlers.

4. I recognize subjects and verbs now.

5. Typed papers make a good impression.

6. I worked until midnight on my paper.

7. The old trunk contained the family photograph albums.

8. We are the product of our environment.

9. Aristotle was the tutor of Alexander the Great.

10. Whitman rewrote <u>Leaves of Grass</u> four times.

☐EXERCISE 9

1. A mature person knows the important from the unimportant.

2. From the kitchen rose the odor of bacon and eggs.

3. The wistful-looking child stood in front of the toy shop.

4. Dad gave his usual admonition about driving carefully.

5. I had no interest in the study of butterflies and beetles.

6. I made the most of every moment of my vacation.

7. She liked his great sense of humor.

8. At that dinner I exceeded the feed limit.

9. I trust her implicitly.

10. Juncos came to my bird feeder all winter.

☐EXERCISE 10

1. The plane soared above the houses.

2. Our journey then led through the magnificent scenery of the Green Mountains.

3. The team fought for the last few points.

4. Swimming is probably the best kind of exercise.

5. Louder and louder grew the sound of the beating drums.

6. The fat man edged his way through the crowd.

7. Climbing to the top of the pyramids requires effort.

8. He carried the ball to the ten-yard line.

9. My relatives live on farms in Illinois.

10. A cold wind swept into the fertile valley.

COMPOUND SUBJECTS AND VERBS

The subject or the verb of a sentence may be compound, or both may be. That is, there may be two or more subjects:

Steve and Mary painted the house.

There may be two or more verbs:

Steve painted the house and planted trees in the yard.

Or there may be two or more subjects and two or more verbs:

Steve and Mary painted the house and planted trees in the yard.

EXERCISES

Underline the subjects once and the verbs twice. Correct your answers by using the perforated answer sheets in the back of the book. Correct each group of ten before going on.

□EXERCISE 1

1. I went outside and walked around the garden.

2. He wore Japanese sandals and kimono but sported a Panama hat.

3. The next morning I awoke at sunrise and looked out at the lake below.

4. That evening we took a boat ride on the lake and later had our supper on the shore under the stars.

5. The next morning I wandered for several miles along the shore and picked up shells of various colors.

6. Magazines and books were on the floor.

7. The captain and the crew escaped in lifeboats.

8. King Arthur and his court gathered in the hall at Camelot.

9. She stopped her car and waited for the truck to pass.

10. He majored in business administration and minored in history.

☐EXERCISE 2

1. Swimming, tennis, and badminton are strenuous sports.

2. The campers and their guide hiked until dusk.

3. The thunder and lightning frightened the children.

4. France and Spain are neighbors.

5. Music, literature, and art are essential for a broad education.

6. I brewed a pot of coffee and carried it through the ankle-deep sand to the men on the levee.

7. One man took the cup from my hand, drank the coffee in a gulp, and held out his cup for more.

8. For three days they filled sacks with dirt and laid them on the top of the levee.

9. They laughed and cried at the same time.

10. She took the box, opened it, and found a Mexican jumping bean.

☐EXERCISE 3

1. He visited the United Nations building and listened to a debate.

2. The student body president and the dean of students conferred about the problem.

3. The incumbent and his opponent engaged in a bitter, no-holds-barred campaign.

4. I reached for my alarm clock and smothered it under my pillow.

5. She looked outside and saw clouds of dust in the street.

6. The old man shuffled along the sidewalk and stopped at intervals for a chat with a neighbor.

7. Lightning struck the cypress in the yard and split it.

8. The wind howled at the tiny house and ripped the yellow rosebush from its trellis.

9. The oboe melody rose harshly and then died away.

10. The amoeba is a transparent little animal no bigger than the period at the end of this sentence.

☐EXERCISE 4

1. She was always agreeable and never offered advice.

2. He and his wife worked their way around the world and then settled down in their hometown.

3. My sister and I wash the dishes every night.

4. The Grapes of Wrath and Of Mice and Men are novels by John Steinbeck.

5. I rose, steadied myself, and launched into my speech.

6. The boys joked with her, challenged her to a race, and then invited her to the festival.

7. The captain walked back and forth on the bridge and gave numerous orders.

8. He pruned the bushes, mowed the lawn, clipped the hedge, and weeded the flower beds all in one evening.

9. They searched the city but found no trace of him anywhere.

10. The men mounted their horses silently and rode off through the screen of snow.

☐EXERCISE 5

1. She worked and saved all her life.

2. The robins and the meadowlarks are the true forerunners of spring.

3. Chemistry and physics were his most difficult subjects.

4. During the night the heavy rain and the wind tore the tent in two.

5. My friends are at their cottages this summer or are at college.

6. Paper and pencils were on the table for the exam.

7. Bears and deer roamed near the cabin all winter.

8. I expected a letter and watched my mailbox daily.

9. The class voted for a party and appointed a committee.

10. During the holidays I failed the swimming exam but had a lot of fun anyway.

□EXERCISE 6

1. The young man opened the door slowly and squinted into the semi-darkness.

2. With the new era, factories and commercialism came into being.

3. He gave me this good-luck charm and asked me to wear it.

4. He and Ellen stopped for us at about seven.

5. A college education broadens and deepens a person's outlook.

6. The child stood in the street and caught falling snowflakes in his open mouth.

7. I wrote out a study schedule and began last night to follow it.

8. For once I did all my homework and felt satisfied.

9. Italian peasants sow wheat between the trunks of the olive trees and string grape vines between the olive branches.

10. Canadians and Americans fought against each other in the War of 1812.

□EXERCISE 7

1. She put the food in the oven and sat down to read the paper.

2. He squared his shoulders and began his speech.

3. The House and the Senate passed the budget bill.

4. I type all my papers and hand them in on time.

5. The sugar maple and the hemlock are both native to Canada.

6. He dashed across the road and clambered down the bank.

7. I walked along the country road and identified some new birds.

8. Great tragedy both sobers and uplifts the human spirit.

9. Jackson and Swenson were winners in the track meet.

10. Jackrabbits, deer, chipmunks, squirrels, and birds fled from the forest fire.

□EXERCISE 8

1. The waxing and the waning of the moon affect the tide.

2. Dr. Salk discovered a vaccine for polio and freed the country from that dread disease.

3. The Arabs marched across the shimmering sand and arrived at last at an oasis.

4. She devoted her life to her family and finally saw them succeed.

5. Queen Victoria ruled Great Britain for sixty-four years and left an indelible stamp upon the age.

6. Disraeli and Gladstone were Victoria's most famous prime ministers.

7. They deserved their popularity and their fame.

8. Leonardo da Vinci designed a flying machine, served as an adviser about the arts of war, and painted some of the world's greatest masterpieces.

9. They tugged and pulled at the boy in the cave-in.

10. Music echoed and reechoed in the narrow chamber.

□EXERCISE 9

1. Jerry and I heard a rock band last night.

2. History and math are my favorite subjects.

3. I sat there and waited my turn.

4. She plays the guitar and sings.

5. In a small Swiss town near the Alps the little train choked feebly and came to a halt.

6. The Essenes apparently lived in caves near a central monastery and held all their goods in common.

7. Cliff swallows circled the roofs and darted into their nests below the eaves.

8. The ship's doctor and the first mate spoke in low tones.

9. White sand, blue sea, and blue sky stretched for miles.

10. The mountains and ice-covered cliffs appeared inaccessible.

□EXERCISE 10

1. The small boy leaned against the side of the barn and whistled on a blade of grass.

2. His mother and grandfather jumped at the sound.

3. The cabdriver pointed to his smashed fender and shouted something in Italian.

4. Sartre and Camus were two existentialist French writers.

5. My time and money went for travel.

6. The car careened around the corner and screeched to a halt.

7. The sun sank slowly in the west and finally disappeared.

8. He made a detailed schedule for each day and followed it.

9. The wind and rain drenched the travelers.

10. The mayor and the property owners opposed the bond issue.

MORE ABOUT VERBS

Sometimes the verb is more than one word. Here are a few of the many forms of the verb *drive:*

drive	has driven	would drive
drives	have been driving	may drive
do drive	have been driven	might drive
does drive	had driven	might have driven
am driving	had been driving	must drive
am driven	had been driven	can drive
drove	shall drive	could drive
did drive	shall be driving	could have driven
was driving	shall be driven	should drive
was driven	will drive	
have driven	will have driven	

There are many more forms. Here are some of these forms in sentences:

Keith drove to the cottage.

Keith should have driven to the cottage last week.

We were driven to the cottage by Keith.

I might have driven to the cottage with him.

Note that words like *not, ever, never, only, always, just* are not part of the verb even though they may be in the middle of the verb.

Keith had never driven to the cottage before.

I had always before driven to the cottage by myself.

She should just have driven around the block.

EXERCISES

Underline the subject once and the verb twice. Be sure to include all parts of the verb. Do only ten sentences at a time before correcting them.

☐EXERCISE 1

1. You must have been working on your vocabulary.

2. Classes were dismissed early during the heat wave.

3. We have been going to the library every evening.

4. Lincoln has been called the best-loved American.

5. Fir trees never lose their needles in winter.

6. Forty men were imprisoned in the mine.

7. She had never before seen such a huge canyon.

8. She did not like lame excuses.

9. The team had played all of the game near our twenty-yard line.

10. I have been working hard this term.

□EXERCISE 2

1. Everyone in the club will be asked to the governor's ball.

2. All football players will be excused from classes on the day of the big game.

3. Somebody will be held responsible for this broken window.

4. Many books have been written about Martin Luther King.

5. She does not like sports.

6. I have never believed in superstitions.

7. I had eaten a chocolate nut sundae before dinner.

8. That pup has been tearing up everything in sight.

9. He had been relying more and more on cramming.

10. He has been having car trouble.

□EXERCISE 3

1. The singer was accompanied by the orchestra.

2. I do not like turnips.

3. The first basketball game will be held on Friday.

4. He was talking loudly in the next room.

5. She had been hoping for an appointment for next week.

6. I have been having a touch of spring fever.

7. He has not been out for football practice lately.

8. He would have called me before noon in that case.

9. His wife had never been in Chicago before.

10. You might offer him some help on his problems.

□EXERCISE 4

1. They should have been asked to the party.

2. They have closed their cottage for the winter.

3. I had been saving that present for her.

4. She should have been doing more work on her math.

5. We have come to the same conclusion.

6. The neighbors must have heard the noise of the party.

7. You should have been told before the last minute.

8. They might have asked him for his advice.

9. By August I will have been working on that job for a year.

10. I had been tutoring him in reading.

□EXERCISE 5

1. The whole class had been studying for the test.

2. I should have told you sooner.

3. In the dictionary, words are divided into syllables.

4. A hyphen is used in compound numbers from twenty-one through ninety-nine.

5. The heat had been oppressive all afternoon.

6. The hot weather had always reminded her of her home in the South.

7. A thousand matches were gleaming in the amphitheater like fireflies.

8. One cello had anticipated the conductor's downbeat.

9. The stadium was rocked with a deafening roar.

10. The farmers had been hoping for rain for three weeks.

□EXERCISE 6

1. Van Allen is known as the discoverer of the doughnut-shaped radiation belts around the earth.

2. The northern lights are perhaps caused by a leakage of radiation particles from the Van Allen belts.

3. The International Geophysical Year was planned for a time of great solar activity.

4. After a heavy fall of snow the cars could not climb the hill.

5. The flamingos were teetering along unsteadily on their spindly legs.

6. He could not reveal the family secret.

7. In an emergency you can depend on her.

8. During the summer I had been studying Spanish.

9. The power of our atomic resources has become tremendous.

10. He had been sleeping for thirteen hours.

□EXERCISE 7

1. For years she had been collecting shells from the beach.

2. She would identify each one carefully.

3. Then she would place it in a cabinet with a neatly typed label.

4. Limpets had always been her favorites.

5. Those shells could be found only at low tide.

6. Others could be found only on the ocean floor.

7. They had not been told about the cost of tuition.

8. He had never thought of it from that angle before.

9. They are waiting beside the gate for their friend.

10. France had acclaimed Lindbergh after his flight.

□EXERCICE 8

1. He had been concerned about her health for some time.

2. No mortar was used by the Egyptians between the great stone blocks of the pyramids.

3. The fashion designers are already decreeing the styles of fall suits.

4. He should have prepared himself for his new job.

5. Shakespeare used several different spellings of his name during his lifetime.

6. Beautiful stained-glass windows were produced in the Dark Ages.

7. My roommate plays his stereo loud.

8. I can't study with so much noise.

9. He has improved in his work.

10. She has been doing her best in that class.

□EXERCISE 9

1. I have been working on my science project.

2. The little bridge does not look strong enough for automobile traffic.

3. She had been working steadily all the morning.

4. They thought nostalgically of their high school days.

5. Van Gogh often applied paint to the canvas with a pallet knife.

6. Seurat, however, would use tiny daubs of pure color.

7. The sound of a church bell had broken the silence of the countryside.

8. My difficulties in English are caused mainly by my poor spelling.

9. During the entire winter they never saw the sun.

10. In the summer the sun never went down.

□EXERCISE 10

1. I have always liked the bread from that bakery.

2. I had never before seen such elaborate snow statues.

3. She had been working for her father all summer.

4. They had never thought of such a thing.

5. They should have reported the accident immediately.

6. The team had been practicing faithfully.

7. The sound of the siren had ended suddenly.

8. The commotion was caused by two people.

9. During the week they had seen two films.

10. The sun went down abruptly behind the mountain.

SUBJECTS NOT IN PREPOSITIONAL PHRASES

We are not going to name many grammatical forms in this workbook, and the only reason we are mentioning prepositional phrases is to get them out of the way. They are always a bother in analyzing sentences. For example, you might have difficulty finding the subject and verb in a long sentence like this:

> Under these circumstances one of the fellows drove to the North Woods during the first week of his vacation.

But if you cross out all the prepositional phrases like this:

> ~~Under these circumstances~~ one ~~of the fellows~~ drove ~~to the North Woods~~ ~~during the first week~~ ~~of his vacation.~~

then you have only two words left—the subject and the verb. And even in short sentences like the following, you might pick the wrong word as the subject if you did not cross out the prepositional phrases first:

> One of my friends lives in Chicago.
> Most of the team went on the trip.

The subject is never in a prepositional phrase. Learn to spot prepositional phrases so that you can get them out of the way. It is much easier to see the structure of a sentence without them.

A prepositional phrase is simply a preposition and the name of something or someone. Read through this list of prepositional phrases so that you will be able to recognize one when you see it:

on the desk	**from** the desk
upon the desk	**to** the desk
above the desk	**into** the desk
over the desk	**toward** the desk
below the desk	**against** the desk
under the desk	**like** the desk
behind the desk	**with** the desk
beneath the desk	**at** the desk
around the desk	**by** the desk
past the desk	**of** them
across the desk	**among** them
through the desk	**without** them
in the desk	**except** them
within the desk	**during** vacation
inside the desk	**before** vacation
beside the desk	**until** vacation

for vacation	**down** the street
after vacation	**along** the street
since vacation	**beyond** the street
up the street	**about** the street

EXERCISES

Cross out the prepositional phrases. Then underline the subject once and the verb twice. Correct each group of ten sentences before going on.

□EXERCISE 1

1. Many ~~of the spectators~~ left ~~at the end~~ ~~of the first half~~.

2. A third of the students really studied for the exam.

3. Most of them passed.

4. After three days in Washington we left for New York.

5. On one side of the lake, a mountain rose abruptly.

6. On the other side was a forest.

7. Both of my sisters graduated from college last year.

8. During the summer I am working with the Parks Department.

9. After the election, people crowded around the information booth.

10. After an early breakfast we started our tour.

□EXERCISE 2

1. "In the spring a young man's fancy lightly turns to thoughts of love."

2. Neither of them had ever been in a play before.

3. In her new position she found challenging problems and congenial associates.

4. Through the streets and up the hill they ran.

5. All of them have their own ski equipment.

6. In my hurry I bumped into two people in the hall.

7. Some of the college students donated to the fund for the refugees.

8. In the evenings she took courses at the college.

9. Millions of American people read the comics.

10. Half of the students bought their tickets early.

☐EXERCISE 3

1. The picture above the fireplace is an heirloom.

2. One of the students finished his term paper last week.

3. Neither of them had ever been to Disneyland.

4. The top of the dam was overhung with trees.

5. The redwing blackbird builds its nest on the ground among the rushes

   beside a stream.

6. In spite of everything we won.

7. One of the judges disagreed with the verdict.

8. Neither of us likes mystery stories.

9. About a week before the election students posted campaign signs on

   buildings and trees around the campus.

10. Each of the players has his own racket.

☐EXERCISE 4

1. One of the best stories in the book is by Edgar Allan Poe.

2. The end of the book was disappointing.

3. During exams all of the students were under the honor code.

4. In the midst of the confusion the key was lost.

5. Neither of them had ever been to Florida.

6. Most of my friends eat their lunch in the cafeteria.

7. Beyond the lake we saw dozens of deer.

8. The total number of known active volcanoes in the world is 455.

9. Three members of the team were on probation.

10. The longest recorded flight of a banded bird during migration is 12,000 miles by an Arctic tern.

□EXERCISE 5

1. Either of the teachers will sign your permit.

2. Any of the club members may invite a guest.

3. Most of us would prefer true and false tests.

4. Under the most trying circumstances she won the match.

5. The exact composition of the core of the earth will be a subject for much conjecture for the next few years.

6. Most of my time after classes and on weekends was spent in the gym.

7. Beneath his gruff exterior we discovered a tender heart.

8. Neither of my best friends has a car.

9. Most of my courses require a lot of homework.

10. After hours of indecision, I finally phoned her.

□EXERCISE 6

1. They gave their opinions on the new law and on the administration in general.

2. The splendid temples at Nikko stand in a grove of giant cryptomeria trees at the top of a hill.

3. All of my classes are held in the main building.

4. One of my most interesting experiences was our trip on a rubber raft down the Colorado River.

5. In most classes a knowledge of English will help.

6. Much of my time is spent in daydreaming.

7. In the last quarter he made a touchdown.

8. Everyone in the bus was annoyed by the noisy child.

9. Men of the eighteenth century would have scoffed at the possibility of many modern inventions.

10. The age of science has, however, encouraged a greater credulity on the part of the public.

□EXERCISE 7

1. Each of the seniors was given a ticket.

2. One of the committee members was absent.

3. In the garden we found a charming reflecting pool.

4. Most of my time was spent in the chemistry lab.

5. Two of my grandparents were pioneers.

6. In a small box at the back of the drawer he had hidden the gold coin.

7. Under one of the plates the lucky number had been placed.

8. One of my friends is studying the archeology of Egypt.

9. The room was filled with a conglomeration of antique furniture.

10. During my stay in Hawaii I learned some of the native songs.

☐**EXERCISE 8**

1. The faces of the gargoyles grinned from the medieval cathedral.

2. In the National Gallery of Art in Washington we saw the famous collection of French Impressionist paintings.

3. During the long afternoon we talked about art.

4. The result of the basketball game was a tie between the two rival teams.

5. Her high school course had provided her with little knowledge of sentence structure.

6. At the edge of the water a sandpiper scuttled away on its long, slender legs.

7. With a slight bow the head waiter indicated an unoccupied table in the corner of the dining room.

8. He stood without a raincoat in the pouring rain.

9. Along the railroad track and between the rails California poppies grew profusely.

10. Throughout the night the stagecoach jolted along the lonely road.

☐**EXERCISE 9**

1. A look of complete bewilderment settled upon the face of the astonished soldier.

2. Toward dawn he yielded to drowsiness.

3. With only six percent of the world's population, America uses sixty percent of the world's resources.

4. The man-made product in greatest abundance today is explosive, obliterative force.

5. The United Nations has received more brickbats than bravos during its more than a quarter century of existence.

6. Yet it remains the only real hope for peace.

7. Dissatisfaction is the spice of life.

8. Through the years Miriam has always been my best friend.

9. During the scuffle the criminal slipped cleverly through an open doorway.

10. The letter for his dad is probably still in his pocket.

□EXERCISE 10

1. I must concentrate at all times upon the job at hand.

2. The end of the term is always hectic.

3. During his early years Picasso burned his sketches for warmth.

4. That book on economics is basic for the course.

5. The statue was reconstructed from excavated fragments of marble.

6. The glass in the medieval stained-glass windows has deep, rich tones.

7. Few forms of sea life can survive in the pounding surf at the base of the cliff.

8. He addressed his caustic comments to the mechanic under the car.

9. Between the two of them they licked the platter clean.

10. The locusts swarmed over the prairie like a thundercloud.

GETTING RID OF RUN-TOGETHER SENTENCES

Any group of words having a subject and verb is a clause. The clause may be independent (able to stand alone) or dependent (unable to stand alone). Every sentence you have worked with so far has been an independent clause because it has been able to stand alone. It has made a complete statement.

If two such independent clauses are written together with no punctuation, or merely a comma, they are called a run-together sentence. We noted some run-together sentences on page 36. Here are some more:

> The girls made the fire the boys cooked the steaks.
> The girls made the fire, the boys cooked the steaks.
> The book was interesting therefore I read it rapidly.
> The book was interesting, therefore I read it rapidly.

Such run-together sentences can be corrected in one of three ways:

1. Make the two independent clauses into two sentences.

> The girls made the fire. The boys cooked the steaks.
> The book was interesting. Therefore I read it rapidly.

2. Separate the two independent clauses with a semicolon. Note the connecting words (underlined) that may come between independent clauses.

> The girls made the fire; the boys cooked the steaks.
> The book was interesting; I read it rapidly.
> The book was interesting; therefore I read it rapidly.
>
> The book was interesting; consequently I read it rapidly.
>
> I worked overtime; thus I finished my project early.
>
> I was late; nevertheless I made the plane.
>
> I was too busy to go; also I wasn't really interested.
>
> I will enjoy the work; furthermore I need the money.
>
> I wrote a thesis statement; then I began my paper.

Other words that may come between independent clauses are *however, likewise, moreover, otherwise.* All of these connecting words require a semicolon in front of them.

3. Connect the two independent clauses with a comma and one of the following connecting words: and, but, for, or, nor, yet, so.

The girls made the fire, but the boys cooked the steaks.
The book was interesting, and I read it rapidly.
I must hurry, or I'll never finish.
I haven't seen that movie, nor do I want to.
He was not outgoing, yet I liked him.

THE THREE WAYS TO PUNCTUATE INDEPENDENT CLAUSES

The book was interesting. I read it rapidly.
The book was interesting; I read it rapidly.
The book was interesting, and I read it rapidly.

Learn these three ways, and you will avoid run-together sentences.

EXERCISES

In each independent clause underline the subject once and the verb twice. Be ready to tell why the sentence is punctuated as it is.

□**EXERCISE 1**

1. His arguments surprised me, for he had always before been a clear thinker.

2. It doesn't matter. Take it all.

3. Thatched houses dotted the landscape, and here and there entire families were working in the wet rice fields.

4. The cabin was cold; moreover there was no firewood.

5. I don't like cooking; nevertheless I can cook a good dinner.

6. The boy ran for miles and never even stopped for breath.

7. The painting was finished; the artist put away his brushes.

8. She isn't coming; she has another appointment.

9. They're from Chicago; they moved here recently.

10. Pronunciation changes over the years, and new words are constantly being added to the language.

□EXERCISE 2

1. The sycamore trees and the old house had shared that yard for over a hundred years, but now the trees were being cut down.

2. Stay a while; it's only nine o'clock.

3. She can't go to the dance, but she isn't sorry.

4. She turned the light switch, but no light came on.

5. The wind began to blow, and suddenly the night was alive and wild.

6. The bus driver had been ten minutes late in starting; moreover he now was hitting all the signals wrong.

7. It was a warm evening; thus she was most uncomfortable in her fur coat.

8. He had always made his own way; he had never had help from anyone.

9. In his day there was no TV; consequently people provided their own entertainment.

10. The door of one of the buildings opened, and a child in tattered clothes came out.

□EXERCISE 3

1. A dry wind blew through the old house, and the shutters rattled.

2. We stopped to build a campfire but had no matches.

3. Not only did we have no matches, but we could not find any stones with which to make a spark.

4. Finally we found some stones, but it took a long time to get a spark.

5. Eventually we had a small fire, but the wood was damp, and it didn't

    burn well.

6. With some pampering the fire finally cooked our food, and we found

    some wild strawberries nearby for dessert.

7. I really prefer a clean kitchen and a table without ants or mosquitoes.

8. You can improve your vocabulary; it just takes determination and prac-

    tice.

9. He always comes late; therefore he often misses the assignment.

10. You're right. This can't go on.

Most of the following sentences are run-together. In each independent clause, underline the subject once and the verb twice. Then separate the two clauses with the correct punctuation—comma, semicolon, or period and capital letter. Remember that the last two ways are interchangeable.

□EXERCISE 4

1. They have moved; they live on the north side of town now.

2. I'd go with you but I'm too tired.

3. Our team lost last night therefore we can't enter the tournament.

4. He listened in class but he didn't take part in class discussions.

5. Set the alarm and I'll study in the morning.

6. At that time my family was living near a small town in the heart of the

    mining country and the hills were full of deserted mine shafts.

7. First the horse trotted then he broke into a gallop.

8. A three-day growth of beard covered his haggard face and his light blue eyes were bloodshot from lack of sleep.

9. He was a strange fellow nevertheless I liked him.

10. That's fine but there's more to it.

□EXERCISE 5

1. I caught a tiny trout and we had it for supper.

2. She didn't like me she said so.

3. Her dress had a wide taffeta skirt and her floppy hat hid her eyes.

4. He gave me a big shove and I fell into the fishpond.

5. Suddenly the string broke the beads bounced over the floor.

6. He studied for his examination all afternoon moreover he didn't even hear his friends outside.

7. Could you understand him I couldn't.

8. Answer the phone it's probably for you.

9. Put on your old coat it's raining.

10. Who are you going with will there be room in the car for me?

□EXERCISE 6

1. The day dawned clear not a cloud was in the sky.

2. He enjoyed camp last summer but he is not going again.

3. We gathered firewood from the nearby woods and the girls unpacked the picnic lunch.

4. Neither of them mentioned the subject again but it was constantly on their minds.

5. His desk was untidy his mind was on other matters.

6. Shut the door it's cold.

7. I can't go to the movie tonight I have too much homework.

8. She's going home she's leaving on the midnight train.

9. Don't worry we'll get there on time.

10. He looked about the camp but he found no traces of recent visitors.

□EXERCISE 7

1. We agreed on the plans then we hurried home.

2. That was a big step forward nevertheless there was still much to do.

3. He worked steadily for two days then he gave up.

4. The house was quiet only the wind outside could be heard.

5. The rain came down in torrents consequently we abandoned our raft and swam for shore.

6. Some people like winter best but I prefer summer.

7. Come in sit down.

8. Read your theme aloud you may catch some foolish errors.

9. You should have come with her you could have stayed at our house.

10. He sent her three pictures of himself but he received none in return.

□EXERCISE 8

1. It was sad news but it was true.

2. Read with your dictionary beside you look up any interesting words.

3. Derivations are important they help you to remember words.

4. Use a new word three times and you won't forget it.

5. Keeping a vocabulary list is helpful then you can review your words.

6. I really wanted to go for I had heard good reports of the play.

7. Where are you going what will you do?

8. He gave up he could go no further.

9. I held her books for her she ran back to the house.

10. Reading improves your understanding of human nature writing improves your understanding of yourself.

□EXERCICE 9

1. A strong wind was blowing our boat nearly capsized.

2. We were grateful to get to shore we should not have ventured out in such weather.

3. He cautiously opened the door and both of them stepped inside.

4. This is a large sunny room you won't find a better one for the price.

5. I took my watch to the jeweler he found the mainspring broken.

6. It's cloudy you must take your umbrella.

7. She turned in anger and left him abruptly.

8. I must go back to work or I won't have a job.

9. He did not say much but his words were kind.

10. You come with us we'll have a good time.

□EXERCISE 10

1. The next day she subscribed for another correspondence course.

2. Are you interested or am I boring you?

3. In youth I wanted to conquer the world now I want only to conquer myself.

4. The barrel-top trunk had belonged to her grandmother the platform rocker had been her aunt's.

5. A flock of Bohemian waxwings descended on her garden and within an hour all the pyracantha berries had disappeared.

6. I've been practicing faithfully and I'm looking forward to our orchestra tour in March.

7. Simplicity was the keynote in her decorating her house was singularly uncluttered and restful.

8. The scrub jay in their backyard became tame it would hop on their patio table and accept bits of food.

9. He was learning the guitar he wasn't, though, quite an Eric Clapton.

10. Dorm life has often been unpleasant nevertheless it has been a good experience.

WRITING YOUR OWN SENTENCES

On a separate sheet write five sentences, each containing two independent clauses. Be sure to punctuate them correctly. Master this section before you go on; it will probably take care of many of your errors in writing.

GETTING RID OF FRAGMENTS

There are two kinds of clauses—independent, which we have just finished studying, and dependent. A dependent clause has a subject and verb just like an independent clause, but it can't stand alone because it begins with a dependent word such as

after	unless
although, though	until
as, as if	what, whatever
because	when, whenever
before	where, wherever
how	whether
if, even if	which, whichever
in order that	while
since	who, whom
that, so that	whose

Whenever a clause begins with one of the above dependent words (unless it is a question, which would never give you any trouble), it is dependent. If we take an independent clause such as

We finished the game.

and put one of the dependent words in front of it, it becomes dependent:

After we finished the game
Although we finished the game
As we finished the game
Because we finished the game
Before we finished the game
If we finished the game
Since we finished the game
That we finished the game
Unless we finished the game
Until we finished the game
When we finished the game
Whether we finished the game
While we finished the game

The clause can no longer stand alone. As you read it, you can hear that it doesn't really say anything. It does not make a complete statement. It leaves the reader expecting something more. **It is a fragment** and must not be punctuated as a sentence.

To correct such a fragment, simply add an independent clause:

After we finished the game, we went to the clubhouse.

While we finished the game, the others waited.
We gave up the court when we had finished the game.
We were happy that we had finished the game.

In other words **EVERY SENTENCE MUST HAVE AT LEAST ONE INDEPENDENT CLAUSE.**

Note in the examples above that when a dependent clause comes at the beginning of a sentence, it is followed by a comma. Often the comma prevents misreading, as in the following sentence:

When he entered, the room became quiet.

Without a comma after *entered*, the reader would read *When he entered the room* before realizing that that was not what the author meant. The comma makes the reading easy. Sometimes if the dependent clause is short and there is no danger of misreading, the comma is omitted, but it is easier and safer simply to follow the rule.

Become familiar with the three groups of connecting words that may come between clauses so that you can avoid run-together sentences and fragments:

GROUP I (BETWEEN INDEPENDENT CLAUSES)

also, consequently, furthermore, however, likewise, moreover, nevertheless, otherwise, therefore, then, thus

They require a semicolon in front of them, or a period and a capital letter.

GROUP II (BETWEEN INDEPENDENT CLAUSES)

and, but, for, or, nor, yet, so

They require only a comma in front of them.

GROUP III (SIGNALING A DEPENDENT CLAUSE)

after, although, though, as, as if, because, before, how, if, even if, in order that, since, that, so that, unless, until, what, whatever, when, whenever, where, wherever, whether, which, whichever, while, who, whom, whose

Use a comma after a dependent clause if it comes at the beginning of a sentence.

Refer to this list when you are writing your papers and want to make sure you don't have any run-together sentences or fragments.

EXERCISES

Write **S** if the clause is independent and therefore a sentence. Add the period after it. Write **F** if the clause is dependent and therefore a fragment not to be punctuated as a sentence. Then add an independent clause to make the fragment into a sentence. If the dependent clause comes first, put a comma after it. When you have finished ten sentences, tear out the answer sheet in the back of the book and correct your sentences before going on.

□EXERCISE 1

_____ 1. The people flocked around the injured man
_____ 2. As the ambulance came racing down the street
_____ 3. When a book is really interesting
_____ 4. Come into the office
_____ 5. As we learned more about the problem
_____ 6. If one lives intelligently
_____ 7. Since you have to catch the five o'clock bus
_____ 8. Because I had so much homework for that evening
_____ 9. Saving is difficult for some people
_____10. We should win this game

□EXERCISE 2

_F_ 1. Unless something goes wrong
_F_ 2. Which I had always wanted to do
_F_ 3. Although he was majoring in engineering
_F_ 4. Even if we decide to go
_F_ 5. Before I had even heard of technology
_F_ 6. While everyone else was studying
_F_ 7. Unless each one brings his own dishes
_S_ 8. She was diligently reading
_F_ 9. Until I got tired of hearing the story
_S_10. Therefore I decided to go

□EXERCISE 3

_S_ 1. I can recommend that book to you
_S_ 2. Then we three made the sandwiches
_S_ 3. The far-off hills are green

___S__ 4. But the news from him was always reassuring
___F__ 5. When he had drunk his fill from the cool spring
___F__ 6. Whether it was from exhaustion or from disease
___F__ 7. While she was in England
___F__ 8. After the sun sank behind the pyramids
___S__ 9. The desert air became cold
___F__10. Even though she is my best friend

□EXERCISE 4

_____ 1. Her affection for her sister had always been great
_____ 2. Newly felled trees were chopped into firewood
_____ 3. Nevertheless she went to live on the coast
_____ 4. When exams are just around the corner
_____ 5. If he could be alone during the day
_____ 6. As I had acquired a great liking for pizza
_____ 7. As he jumped into the air to catch the frisbie
_____ 8. Then there was a sudden rumbling sound
_____ 9. Begin at the beginning
_____10. Since I had had nothing for lunch but a Big Mac

Underline the subject once and the verb twice in both the independent and the dependent clauses. Then put a broken line under the dependent clause.

□EXERCISE 5

1. When it grew too dark for reading, I watched my fellow passengers.

2. He took his van although he really preferred his motorcycle.

3. He was searching for the money that he had dropped in the snow.

4. The book is an account of the expedition of William Beebe to South
   America, where he set up his laboratory for the study of animal life.

5. When the sun went down, the air became cool.

6. As it became dark, we watched the stars.

7. As he dashed after each ball, he grew breathless.

8. Until you understand subjects and verbs, you cannot understand clauses.

9. She sprained her ankle last night while she was skiing.

10. The crowd roared with excitement as one of the Navy players raced down to the goal line.

□EXERCISE 6

1. She chased the puppy through the house until she finally caught him.

2. I should have been waiting still if you had not called.

3. Unless you make an appointment, you cannot see him.

4. One does not do his best when he is tired.

5. This is the third time that I have told him.

6. While Angles, Saxons, and Jutes were still unknown Germanic tribes, their future island home was being made into a province of the Roman Empire.

7. I have always hoped that I could someday go to a Super Bowl championship game.

8. Although I studied hard, I still found the exam difficult.

9. Oliver Twist is a novel of poverty, crime, and injustice as they existed in the London of the nineteenth century.

10. I am not sure that I should go.

Underline the dependent clause.

□EXERCISE 7

1. A large vocabulary is the one characteristic that most often accompanies outstanding success.

2. After I finish college, I shall get a job.

3. A single hydrogen bomb contains more explosive power than all the bombs that were dropped during World War II.

4. Thousands of such bombs are now ready for instant use.

5. Legislators should drop everything that they are doing and do something about the arms race.

6. I refused to go because I had homework to do.

7. I could make good grades if I studied.

8. They were out playing frisbie while he was studying.

9. I couldn't do my math because I didn't have my textbook.

10. Unless you return your library book today, you will have to pay a fine.

□EXERCISE 8

1. The subject that gives me the most trouble is accounting.

2. I admire anyone who is always punctual.

3. From experience you will gain knowledge that you cannot get from books.

4. Make hay while the sun shines.

5. Descartes thought that reason should control man's life.

6. He desperately clung to the side of the boat until his rescuers arrived.

7. They swam for about an hour before they ate their lunch.

8. He never could study while the Monty Python show was on.

9. Her essay would have been better if she had rewritten it.

10. Although he could never walk again, he seemed happy to be alive.

□EXERCISE 9

1. He looked everywhere; he couldn't find the reference material that he needed.

2. The crowd cheered when our football team came onto the field.

3. Don't leave the room until the bell rings.

4. The boy wrote steadily for an hour; he didn't realize that he was writing on the wrong topic.

5. If you are too busy for a vacation, at least get some exercise.

6. While she is away, someone will take her place.

7. When the fire siren sounds, everyone runs to the scene of the fire.

8. If it is nice tomorrow, we will hike up Old Baldy.

9. Although he hates grammar, he is spending hours on it.

10. Because the storm came up so suddenly, we couldn't get to shelter.

□EXERCISE 10

1. Although it snowed yesterday, a large crowd attended the football game.

2. I know what he will say.

3. When he was a child, he pulled weeds in his mother's garden.

4. Her costume, which was homemade, was attractive.

5. While I waited, they finished painting the fence.

6. How do we know that he is telling the truth?

7. The children were delighted with the toys that they received.

8. Although we are the wealthiest member of the United Nations, thirteen

   countries contributed more per capita than we did in 1974.

9. Neither of them has gone on the ski lift yet.

10. While the leaves were still on the trees, we took pictures of the house.

MORE ABOUT FRAGMENTS

We have seen that a dependent clause alone is a fragment. Any group of words that does not have a subject and verb is also a fragment.

Paid no attention to his parents (no subject)
Joe thinking about all his problems (no adequate verb. Although *ing* words look like verbs, no *ing* word alone can ever be a verb of a sentence. It must have another verb in front of it.)
Speeding along the highway (no subject and no adequate verb)
The announcement that we had expected (no verb for the independent clause)

To change these fragments into sentences, we must give each a subject and an adequate verb:

He paid no attention to his parents. (We added a subject.)
Joe was thinking about all his problems. (We put a verb in front of the *ing* word to make an adequate verb.)
Speeding along the highway, he had an accident. (We added an independent clause.)
The announcement that we had expected finally came. (We added a verb for the independent clause.)

Sentence fragments are frequently used in modern writing and are acceptable if the author is using the fragment for a particular purpose. Also in informal letter writing, you may use fragments such as "Haven't had time to write," but in college writing, all fragments should be avoided.

EXERCISES

Write **S** (sentence) or **F** (fragment). Put a period after each sentence, and make each fragment into a complete sentence.

□EXERCISE 1

_F_ 1. When he saw the burglar coming through the window *he yelled.*

_____ 2. After answering the telephone and taking the message

_____ 3. Having washed my only pair of jeans, I crawled into bed

_____ 4. The announcement that there would be no classes on Friday

_____ 5. After falling on the ice and breaking his leg

_____ 6. As in the case of many other inventions

_____ 7. Perspiration is often more needed than inspiration

_____ 8. Swimming along the edge of the river where it was not deep

_____ 9. Having traveled five thousand miles

_____10. The girl making the best of a bad situation

☐EXERCISE 2

_____ 1. After having read several articles in the newspaper about the European situation

_____ 2. Although they had earned enough money to buy a house

_____ 3. Every day with airplanes soaring over the roof of their house

_____ 4. While he climbed to the top of the cliff and looked down over the valley

_____ 5. The coach having given the team a final pep talk

_____ 6. Not having anything to do but rest all day and wait for the phone to ring

_____ 7. While I chopped the kindling wood, they made the fire

_____ 8. The club having postponed the hike until another day

_____ 9. Weakened by lack of food and sleep, we were glad to go home

_____10. Having walked through the forest all day without even a break for lunch

☐EXERCISE 3

_____ 1. At a time when I was too busy to be bothered

_____ 2. My hobby being one which is not expensive

_____ 3. Not even allowing me to give my point of view, he walked away

_____ 4. Having opened the box with great care, I took out the necklace

___S___ 5. Even after I had asked her to be careful

___F___ 6. Didn't even appreciate all she had done for him

___S___ 7. The queer little animal crawling through the bushes

_____ 8. Disappointed by his lack of tact and by his selfishness

___F___ 9. Although neither of us was eager to undertake the job

___S___ 10. An ambitious person makes the most of each opportunity

---

EXERCISE 4

_____ 1. A boring evening in which we did nothing but watch TV

_____ 2. When there is nothing to lose and everything to gain

_____ 3. Since I had reviewed thoroughly, I didn't dread the exam

_____ 4. Being a fellow who always was ready to help

_____ 5. In a beautiful old orchard we ate our picnic lunch

_____ 6. Having been given every opportunity to learn the trade

_____ 7. Each of us hoping that the other would volunteer

_____ 8. Where no man had ever set foot before

_____ 9. The audience applauding wildly and calling for more

_____ 10. Then he suddenly remembered he was supposed to be at a dinner party

---

EXERCISE 5

_____ 1. Give these books to your brother

_____ 2. Although we should not punctuate fragments as sentences

_____ 3. The guys who had been playing baseball all weekend

_____ 4. Seeing that the snowball had broken a window

_____ 5. The boy shook his head

_____ 6. Keep to the right

_____ 7. Which was no easy thing to do

_____ 8. My parents wanting desperately to give me more than they had had

_____ 9. Since I was sure I could get there on time if I kept up my present speed

_____10. Which was more than I was willing to agree to

□EXERCISE 6

_____ 1. As it was snowing, they did not go on the hike

_____ 2. Whether I should continue my education was a problem

_____ 3. A horrible accident which no one will ever forget

_____ 4. Having always done his best in school

_____ 5. The youngster making the most of every opportunity and trying to get ahead

_____ 6. A man whom I had always greatly admired

_____ 7. Her father being a man of very decided opinions

_____ 8. Making the best of everything that happened to him

_____ 9. Hoping all the time that the wind would go down

_____10. A boy who never had had a break in his life

□EXERCISE 7

_____ 1. All of us trying to keep the fire burning and build a shelter

_____ 2. Even though we were told that the game might be postponed

_____ 3. Which is what I had always wanted to do

_____ 4. Finishing the day by vacuuming her room and doing her washing

_____ 5. Probably not because they didn't want to but because they couldn't

_____ 6. During three weeks having barely enough money for eating and sleeping

_____ 7. Facts that no educated person could deny

_____ 8. The witness being something less than trustworthy

_____ 9. The spreading of war news by newspapers and by people who have relatives living in warring nations

_____10. His dream of going into professional football and playing in the Super Bowl

---

□EXERCISE 8

_____ 1. Her roommate still wearing her hair in long braids down her back

_____ 2. Begin at the page that is marked

_____ 3. The same thing over and over, day after day

_____ 4. Whereas another type of person may be very much interested in literature

_____ 5. The fine, fertile farmland that it was years ago

_____ 6. A place where he could feel secure

_____ 7. At least let me carry your books

_____ 8. Don't give up hope yet

_____ 9. Never having had a hundred dollars before

_____10. The room that had meant so much to me as a child

□EXERCISE 9

_____ 1. The little boy shouting excitedly and trying to make us understand

_____ 2. Although someone else might be happy to have such a roommate

———— 3. The girl finding that she was left alone in the huge building and not knowing how to get out

———— 4. That I had intended to do long ago

———— 5. Making no attempt whatever to improve their sordid living conditions

———— 6. Remembering everything he had ever read about haunted houses and wishing that he had at least brought along a flashlight

———— 7. While we watched excitedly and hoped there would be a touchdown in the last few seconds

———— 8. Although rather tired, he decided to finish the journey that night

———— 9. A man who had never wanted for anything in his entire life

————10. It was perfectly obvious that we were lost

□EXERCISE 10

———— 1. Sitting there hoping someone would hear our shouts or see our fire

———— 2. Where he had left it no one knew

———— 3. Unless you want to spend all your time on one subject

———— 4. Give me a nice cold beer and a hamburger

———— 5. Thinking only of himself and how he might win the election

———— 6. Although I have never been known for my acting ability

———— 7. The gracious house that she had so carefully planned

———— 8. I really enjoy classical music

———— 9. Although most of my friends prefer rock

————10. A feeling of belonging that I had always hoped for

WRITING YOUR OWN SENTENCES

Now that you are aware of independent and dependent clauses, you can vary the sentences you write. On a separate sheet write eight sentences,

each containing two independent clauses connected by one of the following words. Be sure to use the correct punctuation—comma or semicolon.

consequently	and
but	thus
therefore	nevertheless
however	then

Now make up eight sentences, **each containing one independent and one dependent clause,** using the following dependent words. If you put the dependent clause first, put a comma after it.

although	unless
after	until
while	because
since	if

Finally, look through the papers that have been handed back to you, and write correctly any fragments or run-together sentences that have been marked.

after we ran, we walk on the serburb.

GETTING RID OF MISPLACED
OR DANGLING MODIFIERS

A modifier explains some word in a sentence, and it should be as close to that word as possible. In the following sentence the modifier is too far away from the word it modifies to make sense.

Leaping across the road we saw two deer.

Was it *we* who were leaping across the road? That is what the sentence says because the modifier *Leaping across the road* is next to *we*. Of course it should be next to *deer*.

We saw two deer leaping across the road.

Now the sentence is clear. The next example has no word at all for the modifier to modify:

At the age of six my family moved to North Dakota.

Obviously the family was not six when it moved. The modifier *At the age of six* is dangling there with no word to attach itself to, no word for it to modify. We must change the sentence so there will be such a word:

At the age of six I moved to North Dakota with my family.

Now the modifier *At the age of six* has a proper word—I—for it to modify. Or we could get rid of the dangling modifier by turning it into a dependent clause:

When I was six, my family moved to North Dakota.

Here the clause has its own subject—I—and there is no chance of misunderstanding the sentence.

The following sentences contain similar dangling modifiers—dangling because there is no word for them to modify:

Looking down over the valley, a wisp of smoke appeared. (Was the wisp of smoke looking down over the valley? Who was?)
After running six blocks, the bus pulled away as I reached it. (Had the bus run six blocks? Who had?)

Rewrite each of the above two sentences in two ways to get rid of the dangling modifier. Cover the right-hand column on the next page until you have done your rewriting.

1. First change each sentence so there is a word for the modifier to modify:

_____   Looking down over the
_____   valley, I saw a wisp
_____   of smoke appear.

_____   After running six blocks,
_____   I saw the bus pull away
_____   as I reached it.

2. Then turn the dangling modifier into a dependent clause:

_____   While I looked down
_____   over the valley, a
_____   wisp of smoke appeared.

_____   After I had run six
_____   blocks, the bus pulled
_____   away as I reached it.

Either way of getting rid of the dangling modifier makes the sentence clear.

EXERCISES

Most—but not all—of these sentences contain misplaced or dangling modifiers. Some you may correct simply by shifting the modifier so that it will be next to the word it modifies. Others you will need to rewrite. Since there is more than one way to correct each sentence, your way may be as good as the one in the back of the book.

☐EXERCISE 1

1. You will enjoy looking at the pictures that you took years later.

2. Sound asleep on the front porch I came across my grandfather.

3. Crawling across the dusty road I saw a furry little caterpillar.

4. Taking her in his arms the moon hid behind a cloud.

5. Thoughtfully beginning to dress, the new blue jeans and clean shirt reminded him that at last he had a job.

6. To get the most out of college, one should follow a time budget.

7. Working really hard, the term paper was finished in six hours.

8. When ten years old my mother gave me a ring.

9. After asking three or four people, the right road was finally found.

10. Crashing to the ground, I was sure I saw an airplane.

☐EXERCISE 2

1. After cleaning my room, my dog wanted to go for a walk.

2. After graduating from grammar school his mother took him to Europe.

3. Bored and tired, the lecture went over my head.

4. Trembling from fright, the child ran to her mother's arms.

5. After playing frisbie all evening, my English paper did not get finished.

6. Slamming the door he marched out of the house.

7. Leaning against the barn I saw the broken ladder.

8. After watching TV all evening, the dirty dishes were still on the table.

9. At the age of six my grandfather paid us a visit.

10. Looking out the window, the plane could be seen.

☐EXERCISE 3

1. Badly in need of a bath I brought the dog into the laundry room.

2. I was hit by a boy in the face with a pomegranate skin.

3. Dressed in a long blue evening gown, he thought she had never looked prettier.

4. While running down the beach, I stubbed my toe and fell headlong.

5. Darting here and there through the bushes, we watched the first spring warblers.

6. Crying pitifully, I stopped and talked to the child.

7. Sitting beside the hotel window, the entire ski tournament could be seen.

8. We saw the rabbit run by fleeing from the dogs.

9. Stepping on the gas, the car shot forward.

10. Hoping it would quit raining by the next day, the picnic was postponed.

□EXERCISE 4

1. While driving along in the car, a deer ran across the road.

2. Falling from the top of the Empire State Building we could see little white pieces of paper.

3. While on a two-week vacation, the office had to take care of itself.

4. I saw that the murderer had been captured in the evening paper.

5. Driving as fast as possible, the hospital was finally reached.

6. I bought a car from a used-car dealer with a leaky radiator.

7. The fans must have had to have a lot of blankets sitting out there in the stadium.

8. Apologetically the food was placed before us.

9. While talking to one another, the ideas became clear.

10. Dad urged me to finish my college career with threats and promises.

□EXERCISE 5

1. While tobogganing down the hill, a huge bear came out of the woods.

2. Gleaming red in the sunlight, he suddenly noticed a stop sign.

3. I watched a monkey running up a coconut tree.

4. The monkey watched us peeling a banana in the cage.

5. Screaming and kicking, I tried to quiet the child.

6. We watched the rabbits nibbling at the new-mown clover.

7. Rocking back and forth, her thoughts remained unspoken.

8. While she was eating dinner, a special delivery letter arrived.

9. Having worked hard all day, the lawn had to go without mowing.

10. Suddenly becoming frightened, the house seemed full of noises.

□EXERCISE 6

1. Because of going to too many parties, my term paper was late.

2. Having narrowly missed being run over, I gave the child some advice about crossing streets.

3. Groping around in the dark for the switch, the coffee table was overturned.

4. Having finished eating, the table lay bare.

5. While hiking up the mountain, we saw three porcupines.

6. Being very tired Mother told me I didn't need to help with the dishes.

7. Lying there on the beach in the sun, schoolwork didn't seem important.

8. Wagging his tail excitedly, the dog seemed to be as pleased as the boy.

9. Moving slowly down the street we saw the parade.

10. Looking at the dress closely, I saw that the material was coarse.

□EXERCISE 7

1. Putting on the brakes quickly, the car screeched to a stop.

2. Consulting the Lost and Found section of the paper, the dog was soon safe at home again.

3. Barking furiously, the puppy ran after the old man.

4. There was a spot on her new dress that could not be removed.

5. Skidding to a stop, the old lady barely missed being hit by our car.

6. By concentrating intently, I at last understood the meaning of the paragraph.

7. I lost a pen out of my briefcase that did not belong to me.

8. I decided to give the clothes to a charity that I had no use for.

9. Although almost eight years old, he refused to turn his car in on a newer model.

10. We noticed a small flower in the lapel of his coat that she no doubt had given him.

□EXERCISE 8

1. Purring contentedly, I saw the cat in my armchair.

2. A son was born to Mr. and Mrs. N. L. Smith weighing eight pounds.

3. Being a bore, I don't enjoy his company.

4. Except when pickled, I don't care for cucumbers.

5. Discouraged, the book and all the notes fell to the floor.

6. Almost too excited to eat, the letter was read over and over.

7. Jumping the little creek, her eyes fell on a large bed of violets.

8. He ran up the steps and into the deserted house shivering with cold.

9. We are having a series of lectures on religions of the world which will end May 30.

10. She put the sandwiches back in the bag that she had not eaten.

□EXERCISE 9

1. After driving a thousand miles, her children welcomed her home.

2. At the age of three my father took me to the city for the first time.

3. Having been born and raised in the country, the old cookstove naturally appeals to me.

4. Excited and eager to go, the bus was in front of the building waiting for us.

5. The house is surrounded by a grove of catalpa trees where I was born.

6. After a three-year absence, the trees were full grown.

7. Unwrapping gift after gift, the puppy had a great time playing with all the tissue paper.

8. Zooming down the hill, the tree was struck with a bang.

9. After eating lunch hurriedly, the two taxis then started for Yosemite.

10. Discouraged, the park seat made a good resting-place for the tramp.

□EXERCISE 10

1. The youngster went careening down the driveway just as we arrived on a scooter.

2. Quietly munching hay I watched the horses in the pasture.

3. The little black dog followed him wagging his tail.

4. The bride was tripped by the rug marching down the aisle.

5. While talking on the phone the cake burned.

6. With love and care I realized my parents had raised me the best they could.

7. Lincoln Park is the most interesting park in the city that I have seen.

8. She was engaged to a man with a Cougar named Smith.

9. At the age of fourteen my sister was born.

10. We gave all the food to the dog that we didn't want.

GETTING RID OF FAULTY REFERENCES

When you write a sentence, *you* know what it means, but your reader may not. What does this sentence mean?

John told his father he would have to take the car to the garage.

Who would have to take the car? We don't know what word the pronoun *he* refers to, whether to John or to father. The sentence might mean

John said that his father would have to take the car to the garage.

or

John told his father he was planning to take the car to the garage.

A simpler way to get rid of such a faulty reference is to use a direct quotation:

John said to his father, "I will have to take the car to the garage."

Here is another sentence with a faulty reference:

I have always been interested in nursing and finally have decided to become one.

Decided to become a nursing? There is no word for *one* to refer to. We need to write

I have always been interested in nursing and finally have decided to become a nurse.

Another kind of faulty reference is a *which* clause that refers to an entire idea:

No one could tell him where the bike had been left which made him angry.

Was he angry because no one could tell him or because the bike had not been left in its proper place? The sentence should read

It made him angry that the bike had not been left in its place.

or

It made him angry that no one could tell him where the bike had been left.

EXERCISES

Most of the following sentences are not clear because we do not know what word the pronoun refers to. Rewrite each sentence, making the meaning clear. Remember that using a direct quotation is often the easiest way to clarify a pronoun reference. Since there are more ways than one to rewrite each sentence, yours may be as good as the one given on the answer sheet. Just ask yourself whether the meaning of the sentence is perfectly clear.

□EXERCISE 1

1. I put the omelet on the table, took off my apron, and began to eat it.

2. The government has established schools where they learn cooking, interior decorating, and household management.

3. I decided not to get a summer job which annoyed my family.

4. She asked her sister why she wasn't invited to the party.

5. Jay's father let him take his new tennis racket to school.

6. She tried to persuade her roommate to wear her red dress.

7. The president told the dean he had been too lenient.

8. To be a good fraternity brother you must cooperate with any project they undertake.

9. The teachers established a play center where they can spend their leisure.

10. Ray told the professor that his watch was wrong.

□EXERCISE 2

1. When I picked up the dog's dish, it began to bark.

2. I have always been interested in coaching football ever since I was in high school, and now I have decided to become one.

3. She served me a pizza, which was cold.

4. I enjoyed my month in Japan. They are an artistic people.

5. The chairwoman asked her to keep her secret from the others.

6. Sandra told Janice that she was wasting her time studying music.

7. I have a pair of glasses, but my eyes are so good that I don't use them except for reading.

8. Although I had never been fishing before, I caught one immediately.

9. She likes to swim; in fact she spends most of her summer doing it.

10. She is good in her studies although not very good in sports. This is why she was chosen student body president.

□EXERCISE 3

1. He asked his boss whether he would have to make out a claim sheet concerning the accident.

2. We couldn't find the cake plate and realized the children must have eaten it.

3. Her mother told her she would have to be more considerate.

4. The naturalist showed us his collection of birds' nests and told us how they build them.

5. I have adjusted the steering wheel, and you can take it home anytime.

6. After I had read the story of Lindbergh's life, I decided that that is what I want to be.

7. He asked the man to come back when he had time to talk.

8. When Jerome talked to his father, he was very angry.

9. They refused to promote the new invention which hurt their business.

10. His father told him he would have to try to get a more modern view.

□EXERCISE 4

1. Andy told his brother that his car had a flat tire.

2. I enjoy prizefights and would like to be one if I could.

3. She told her daughter she had always been a good cook.

4. In China their main food is rice.

5. I didn't follow my father's advice which turned out to be wise.

6. Mrs. Smith told Mrs. Brown that her dog was in her yard.

7. The cars whizzed past, but they didn't even look my way.

8. As soon as I approached the robin's nest, it flew away.

9. Sarah had lost the term paper which she had written which wasn't easy to explain to the instructor.

10. She told her roommate she was spending too much time going to parties.

□EXERCISE 5

1. He told his dad he needed a new suit.

2. He asked his professor why he couldn't understand the essay.

3. He told his roommate that he was a time waster.

4. Hawaii is a beautiful state where they allow no billboards.

5. My math teacher gave me a low grade because I was really poor in it.

6. He told his father he ought to wash the car.

7. I walked into the room, climbed on the ladder, and began to paint it.

8. The professor told him that his article was going to be published.

9. Ben told his father he ought to get a refund for the faulty tire.

10. When I opened the door of the birdcage, it flew out.

☐**EXERCISE 6**

1. I've been trying to decide what trip to take which isn't easy.

2. It would be cold in New England at this time of year which I don't like.

3. He asked the mechanic why he was having trouble.

4. As soon as Dad had put in the new battery, I went whizzing off in it.

5. He complained to his father that his car was an antique.

6. I have always liked French Provincial furniture and have finally decided to buy one.

7. She told her instructor she didn't understand what she was saying.

8. Al told Mark he was extravagant.

9. She told her mother she thought she needed a physical checkup.

10. We had to read only two textbooks which I really liked.

☐**EXERCISE 7**

1. When I moved the child's tricycle, it screamed.

2. In Huxley's Brave New World he describes many things that have come true today.

3. Lauren told her mother that her dresses were all dated.

4. I stopped at the old Wiley Schoolhouse, which has been designated as a state historical site.

5. The car hit the bridge railing, but it was not damaged.

6. When I went to the sorority rush party, I was impressed with how friendly they were.

7. We spent our vacation in Nassau, where we found their climate delightful.

8. I thought he would phone, and I waited all evening for it to ring.

9. I've decided to save all my money for a trip which won't be easy.

10. He told his twin brother that he had been at fault.

□EXERCISE 8

1. Because he missed the curve, his motorcycle swerved into the side of a house, but it wasn't damaged.

2. As I approached the baby's playpen, it began to cry.

3. As soon as the fender was repaired, I drove it home.

4. The instructor told him that he did not understand the poem.

5. His father told him he thought he should carry more insurance.

6. Yesterday I turned in a paper which came back with an A grade.

7. I liked California except that they have a lot of smog.

8. She told her visitor to come back when she had had more time to study the project.

9. When the boss talked with Mac, he was really despondent.

10. She told her roommate that her stereo needed a new needle.

□EXERCISE 9

1. When I praised the child's finger painting, it was pleased.

2. They offered me a job which pleased me.

3. The instructor told him that his explanation had been faulty.

4. As I tried to attach the dog's leash, it jumped away.

5. There were only six students in that class which I really liked.

6. I refused to follow his suggestion which turned out to be a good thing.

7. Her counselor told her she needed more time to think about the question.

8. I'm taking lessons in golf, which is my favorite sport.

9. She told her mother she needed to be positive before making such a big decision.

10. We couldn't find a single bottle and blamed Mike for drinking all of them.

□EXERCISE 10

1. The chairman asked him to reconsider his statement.

2. When her roommate came in at four a.m., she was crying.

3. His dad told him he would have to be more generous with his time.

4. She showed us her shell collection and explained how they live in them.

5. The parents take turns at the playground where they can use the slides, swings, and teeter-totters.

6. David told his instructor he was confused about the novel.

7. They refused to give me any more money which was just what I needed.

8. The salesman told his supervisor he had been negligent in his job.

9. They asked me to serve on the committee which I thought was unnecessary.

10. When she talked with her mother, she asked her to have a little better sense of humor in the future.

MAKING SUBJECTS, VERBS, AND PRONOUNS AGREE

All parts of a sentence should agree. In general if the subject is singular, the verb should be singular; if the subject is plural, the verb should be plural.

Each of the boys has his own room.

Over by the fireplace were two chairs.

There were two places set at the long table.

The following words are singular and almost always take a singular verb:

(*one* words)	(*body* words)	
one	nobody	each
anyone	anybody	either
someone	somebody	neither
everyone	everybody	

One of my friends is a freshman.

Each of the students is responsible for one report.

Either of the girls is a good choice.

Sometimes, though, the verb agrees with the *intent* of the subject rather than with its actual form.

Neither of them were in. (The sentence means that both were not in.)

Such exceptions to the rule occur more often in conversation than in writing.

Not only should subject and verb agree. A pronoun, too, should agree with the word it refers to. If that word is singular, the pronoun should be singular; if that word is plural, the pronoun should be plural.

Each of the boys has *his* own room.

The pronoun *his* refers to the singular subject *Each* and therefore is singular.

Both of the boys have *their* own rooms.

The pronoun *their* refers to the plural subject *Both* and therefore is plural.

Modern usage, however, allows many exceptions to this rule, especially in conversation. When the word referred to is plural in *meaning*, even though singular in form, a plural pronoun may be used.

> *Everybody* took off *their* hats as the parade went by.
> *Everyone* was here, but *they* all went home early.
> *Everybody* has *their* faults.

In all of these sentences the intent of the subject is to show that many people were involved. Therefore the plural pronouns are used, although of course the singular forms would be grammatically correct.

The plural pronouns *they* and *them* are being used more and more frequently to avoid using the awkward *he/she* and *him/her*, particularly in conversation.

> If *anyone* is ready, *they* can go in my car. (Less awkward than the grammatically correct *he or she can go in my car.*)
> If *anybody* calls, tell *them* I've left. (Less awkward than the grammatically correct *tell him or her I've left.*)

Usage changes, and today strict rules of grammar are not always followed. But be sure to stick with the rules until you are told that an exception to a rule is now considered acceptable. In writing it is usually simpler and safer to stick with the rules.

The following "group" words take a singular verb if you are thinking of the group as a whole, but they may take a plural verb if you are thinking of the individuals in the group:

group	band	heap
committee	flock	lot
crowd	class	audience
team	dozen	jury
family	kind	herd
number	public	

The group *is* planning a show. . . . . The group *are* giving their reports.
My family *is* behind me. . . . . My family *are* all scattered.
The number present *was* small. . . . . A number *are* going to the rally.
A dozen *is* enough. . . . . A dozen *are* going.
A lot *was* accomplished. . . . . A lot *were* late to class.

Here are some subject-verb pairs that you can *always* be sure of:

you were	(**never** you was)
we were	(**never** we was)
he doesn't	(**never** he don't)
she doesn't	(**never** she don't)
it doesn't	(**never** it don't)

Making subjects and verbs agree is one of the biggest problems of those who have grown up speaking a dialect other than Standard English. Here is a table showing the endings of a few common verbs in Standard English. Most verbs have endings like the first verb, *walk*, but many are irregular. Only three irregular verbs—*be, have,* and *do*—are given here, but they will give you a start. If you have been speaking a dialect other than Standard English, memorize these verb forms and practice using them so that your writing will conform to the written English used all over the United States.

STANDARD ENGLISH

Regular Verbs

Present		Past	
I, you, we, they	walk	I, you, we, they	walked
he, she, it	walks	he, she, it	walked

Irregular Verbs

I	am	I, he, she, it	was
you, we, they	are	we, you, they	were
he, she, it	is		

I, you, we, they	have	I, you, we, they	had
he, she, it	has	he, she, it	had

I, you, we, they	do	I, you, we, they	did
he, she, it	does	he, she, it	did

EXERCISES

Cross out the prepositional phrases so that you can find the subject of the sentence. Then underline the correct verb in the parentheses. In some sentences you will also need to underline the correct pronoun. Use the correct grammatical form even though an alternate form may be acceptable in conversation.

□EXERCISE 1

1. Each of the boys (is are) making (his their) special gift for Mickey.
2. The reason for my failure (was were) my absences from class.
3. It (doesn't don't) make any difference to me.
4. She (walk walked) up to me yesterday and (ask asked) a question.
5. Some of those tricks (is are) easy.
6. It had been two years since we (was were) there.
7. There (is are) three apples in a dish on the table.
8. Both of the boys (was were) skating on the neighborhood rink.
9. She (goes go) to the new junior college, (doesn't don't) she?
10. (Doesn't Don't) he plan to make the trip?

□EXERCISE 2

1. Each of the stamps (was were) distinctive in (its their) own way.
2. Each of my sisters (has have) (her their) own apartment.
3. A number of us (has have) already made reservations.
4. Ice skating, like tap dancing, (requires require) strong muscles, (doesn't don't) it?
5. There (was were) ten people waiting in line, and we (was were) at the end.
6. One of us (is are) making a mistake.
7. She (doesn't don't) even want to walk along the beach.
8. Several of the seniors (has have) been chosen.
9. Each of the lessons (presents present) a different problem.
10. I never knew you (was were) from Missouri.

□EXERCISE 3

1. Everyone in the chorus (is are) ready.
2. Peggy and Jill (was were) home for the holidays.
3. Anyone who has finished all (his their) projects (is are) eligible for promotion.
4. He (doesn't don't) even try to get along with his parents.
5. Each of us (has have) been at fault.
6. Each of the boards (was were) an inch and a half wide.

7. Most of the stories in the little magazine (contains contain) some humor.
8. Each of the buildings (exhibits exhibit) a different style of architecture.
9. All of the buildings on our campus (is are) Modern Gothic.
10. Each of the buildings (was were) built to conform to the master plan.

□EXERCISE 4

1. I am sure she (doesn't don't) want to go.
2. All of the children (was were) watching the magician with open mouths.
3. We slept late this morning because we (was were) up late last night.
4. All of our buildings (is are) fireproof.
5. I thought you (was were) there.
6. Nobody in our class (is are) working on (his their) project yet.
7. Somebody in the crowd (was were) shouting for a doctor.
8. All of the others (was were) exhausted, but she (walk walked) still farther.
9. Everyone in our dorm (is are) going to the game.
10. One of my friends (is are) going to a cooking class.

□EXERCISE 5

1. The twins and I (am are) planning to work at the polling booth.
2. We (was were) there until two o'clock, and everybody (was were) having a good time.
3. (Doesn't Don't) he ever study?
4. When we ran out of gas, we (was were) miles from town.
5. He (doesn't don't) understand the difference between sentences and sentence fragments.
6. Nobody (is are) going now.
7. We (walk walks) to the campus every morning; we even (walk walked) through the snow all last winter.
8. In front of the house (was were) two policemen.
9. A box of oranges (was were) sent to our house by mistake.
10. There (was were) packages from all of her friends.

□EXERCISE 6

1. They (is are) crazy; they (expect expects) to get in free.
2. I (pass passed) my history exam, and I (refuse refuses) to worry any more about it.
3. I thought you (was were) going home this weekend.
4. Every one of the girls (cooks cook) good meals.
5. Everybody in the crowd (was were) glad to see the sun.
6. Why (doesn't don't) he go out for football?
7. There (remains remain) a number of insoluble problems.

8. I'm sure she (doesn't don't) believe all those compliments.
9. I (use used) to play the piano, but now I (hasn't haven't) the time to practice.
10. Both of them (has have) grown up among intellectuals.

□EXERCISE 7

1. It (doesn't don't) matter now.
2. We (want wanted) to go skiing last week, but we (was were) too busy.
3. Few of us (is are) that studious.
4. A number of the delegates (is are) voting against him.
5. There (has have) been many reasons for my inability to concentrate.
6. One of my aunts (is are) coming here next week.
7. (Doesn't Don't) he even want to vote?
8. When I (talk talked) to him yesterday, he (ask asked) me to stop at his house, and he (cook cooked) dinner for me.
9. It was raining the whole time that we (was were) there.
10. He (doesn't don't) know much about the candidates.

□EXERCISE 8

1. (Wasn't Weren't) you surprised at her answer?
2. There never (is are) enough books to go around.
3. The reason that we (was were) late was that our car wouldn't start.
4. You (was were) in good form the last half of the game.
5. Most of the students (was were) there for the free movie.
6. I (wonder wonders) why he (drop dropped) his math course.
7. It (doesn't don't) matter whether you go or not.
8. Everybody on the committee (is are) in favor of an early date for the prom.
9. I'm sure they (was were) happy to see you.
10. (Doesn't Don't) she enjoy her new position?

□EXERCISE 9

1. Last week we (move moved) to our new house which (seem seems) very comfortable.
2. That house (fulfill fulfills) my mother's dreams because the yard (contain contains) many trees.
3. He (doesn't don't) work very hard.
4. You (was were) there too, (wasn't weren't) you?
5. You (walk walked) yesterday as if you (was were) lame.
6. You (walk walks) today as if you (is are) lame.
7. Each of the twins (has have) (his their) own style of swimming.

8. (Doesn't Don't) he have any money?
9. He (scare scared) them with his fast driving.
10. Each of the novels in the series (has have) (its their) own specially de-signed cover.

□EXERCISE 10

1. That book that we (discuss discussed) in class yesterday (interest in-terests) me.
2. The instructor (analyze analyzed) it and (use used) some examples from it.
3. It really (impress impressed) me.
4. (Doesn't Don't) she live here anymore?
5. Ruby (walk walks) like a dancer.
6. Sports (fascinate fascinates) me, and I (want wants) to become a coach.
7. I (follow follows) all the news about football and (hope hopes) someday to coach football.
8. That street (has have) played an important part in my life.
9. (Was Were) you there when she (play played) her guitar?
10. We (canvass canvassed) for the Heart Fund in our dorm last week.

WRITING YOUR OWN SENTENCES

On a separate sheet write five sentences using verbs that you know you some-times use incorrectly.

CHOOSING THE RIGHT PRONOUN

Of the many kinds of pronouns, the following cause the most difficulty:

SUBJECT GROUP	NONSUBJECT GROUP
I	me
he	him
she	her
we	us
they	them

A pronoun in the Subject Group may be used in two ways:

1. as the subject of a verb:

> *He* is my brother. (*He* is the subject of the verb *is.*)
> *We* girls gave a party. (*We* is the subject of the verb *gave.*)
> He is taller than *I*. (The sentence is not written out in full. It means "He is taller than I am." *I* is the subject of the verb *am.*)
> She plays as well as *he*. (The sentence is not written out in full. It means "She plays as well as he does." *He* is the subject of the verb *does.*)

2. as a word that means the same as the subject:

> That boy in the blue jeans is *he*. (*He* is a word that means the same as the subject *boy*. Therefore the pronoun from the Subject Group is used.)
> It was *she* all right. (*She* means the same as the subject *It*. Therefore the pronoun from the Subject Group is used.)

> Modern usage allows some exceptions to this rule, however. *It is me* and *it is us* (instead of the grammatically correct *It is I* and *it is we*) are now established usage, and *it is him, it is her*, and *it is them* are widely used, particularly in informal speech.

Pronouns in the Nonsubject Group are used for all other purposes. The following pronouns are not subjects, nor are they words that mean the same as subjects. Therefore they come from the Nonsubject Group.

> He came with Lynn and *me*. (A good way to tell which pronoun to use is to leave out the extra name: He came with *me*.)
> We saw Lynn and *him* last night. (We saw *him* last night.)
> He gave *us* boys a pony. (He gave *us* a pony.)
> He gave Stan and *them* some tickets. (He gave *them* some tickets.)

EXERCISES

Underline the correct pronoun. Use the form from the subject group only if the pronoun is the subject or is a word that means the same as the subject. Correct your answers ten at a time.

□EXERCISE 1

1. This is strictly between you and (I me).
2. We gave Carla and (he him) a large brown dog for Christmas.
3. Dad's eyes were very thin in disapproval of my brother and (I me).
4. That is a question for you and (he him) to decide.
5. (He Him) and (I me) went skiing after school.
6. At the end of the semester he asked if he could get a ride home with my sister and (I me).
7. My mother had said good-bye to my brother and (I me).
8. It was a good thing for (we us) fellows that we had studied.
9. You should have heard the conversation between Noel and (I me).
10. We saw (she her) and Nick going into the theater.

□EXERCISE 2

1. They left the dishes for Sis and (I me) to do.
2. The trunk was given to (us we) three fellows as a joke.
3. There's difficulty between (he him) and his parents.
4. Did you see (he him) and Alice dancing the hustle last night?
5. No one could be more of a clown than (he him).
6. It was a close game between my cousin and (I me).
7. The director asked (we us) girls to help serve.
8. I saw Karl and (she her) last night after the movie.
9. No one could be better prepared for the exam than (he him).
10. (We Us) fellows had seldom given a thought to study.

□EXERCISE 3

1. It was up to my roommate and (I me) to alert the gang.
2. Mother brought my brother and (I me) gifts from Mexico.
3. (We Us) fellows hadn't even tried out for track.
4. Mother laid down the law to my brother and (I me).
5. The streetcar trundled off, leaving Dan and (I me) standing bewildered on the corner.
6. The club finally dropped my brother and (I me) from membership.
7. The committee asked (he him) and the treasurer to plan the drive for funds.

8. The first round in the tournament eliminated (he him) and Jack.
9. It cost Don and (I me) two dollars apiece to make that long-distance call.
10. The next day they left (she her) and the nurse alone with my grand-father.

□EXERCISE 4

1. The gang came running after Tim and (I me).
2. They sent a telegram to (she her) and her brother.
3. They wanted to know whether (she her) and her brother would come to the wedding.
4. This must be a secret between (we us) two.
5. I have been there oftener than (he him).
6. He left the decision up to (we us) fellows.
7. While we were traveling in Mexico, time meant nothing to Lou and (I me).
8. May (we us) girls help?
9. We've never before had a forward as good as (she her).
10. (We Us) children had never been left alone before.

□EXERCISE 5

1. He tried to persuade Mother to go along with (we us) girls.
2. Dad gave my brother and (I me) motorcycles for Christmas.
3. I don't think there is much in common between (he him) and his father.
4. I'm surely as smart as (he him).
5. (We Us) girls did the decorating.
6. The decorating was left to (we us) girls.
7. My aunt asked my sister and (I me) to go with her to St. Louis.
8. My aunt asked whether my sister and (I me) would like to go to the carnival.
9. It was a joke among (we us) guys.
10. I hope that my boyfriend and (I me) will be invited.

□EXERCISE 6

1. Alec and (he him) are my best friends.
2. She asked Allan and (I me) to her party.
3. Mother asked Sis and (I me) to do the dishes.
4. I gave all the tickets to (she her) and her roommate to sell.
5. You should invite (he him) and his girl friend.
6. She was more to blame than (he him).
7. The dean gave my roommate and (I me) a cold look.
8. The dean said my roommate and (I me) should have used better judgment .

9. They left plenty of ice cream for Phil and (I me) even if we were an hour late.
10. That is a problem for you and (I me) to decide.

□EXERCISE 7

1. Why didn't she ask Paul and (he him) to come?
2. I am older than (he him).
3. (They Them) and (I me) went bowling.
4. I told Louise about the plan for Gail and (she her).
5. Leave it to (we us) girls.
6. I wonder why (he him) and his brother don't play football.
7. She is far better in math than (I me).
8. (We Us) fellows voted against the plan.
9. We should be able to sell more than (they them).
10. Finally (we us) boys decided that something had to be done.

□EXERCISE 8

1. (Alec and I, Me and Alec) followed the others in Alec's car.
2. Everyone thought Alec and (I me) would get there last.
3. None of (we us) guys had ever been on that road before.
4. No one could decide that problem except my father and (I me).
5. My father and (I me) sat down to talk it over.
6. Nobody is as level-headed as (he him).
7. My grandparents sent a gift to my brother and (I me).
8. My sister is a harder worker than (I me).
9. It was left to the counselor and (I me) to assign the tents.
10. If I were (he him), I'd admit my guilt.

□EXERCISE 9

1. The noise was blamed on my roommate and (I me).
2. Actually he was more to blame than (I me).
3. Some of (we us) freshmen are always being blamed for something.
4. My brother and (I me) have an agreement between us.
5. He always has been a better trackman than (I me).
6. (We Us) guys have really been practicing for the meet.
7. Between you and (I me), I think our team will win.
8. The coach has left it to Larry and (I me) to arrange the rides.
9. The score was a tie between (them they) and (we us).
10. They gave (we us) fellows a good match.

□EXERCISE 10

1. The women expected (we us) men to do all the cooking for the camp.

2. Most of the lecture seemed to be directed at (we us) freshmen.
3. The orchestra director said that he had never had a better flute player than (he him).
4. Kent's new girl made a good impression on my parents and (I me).
5. Kent and (her she) are going to be married in the spring.
6. (Me and my kid brother, My kid brother and I) will be ushers at the wedding.
7. My cousin is smarter than (I me), but she doesn't work as hard.
8. Consequently I usually get better grades than (her she).
9. They left it up to Joan and (I me) to plan the refreshments.
10. We had some disagreements, but there were no hard feelings between (we us) two.

WRITING YOUR OWN SENTENCES

On a separate sheet write five sentences using pronouns you may have had trouble with.

USING PARALLEL CONSTRUCTION

Your writing will be clearer if you use parallel construction. That is, when you make any kind of list, put the items in similar form. If you write

I enjoy *swimming, skiing,* and *to hunt.*

the sentence lacks parallel construction. The items do not all have the same form. But if you write

I enjoy **swimming, skiing,** and **hunting.**

then the items are parallel. They all have the same form. They are all *ing* words. Or you could write

I like **to swim, to ski,** and **to hunt.**

Again the sentence uses parallel construction because the items all have the same form. They all use *to* and a verb. Here are some more examples. Note how much easier it is to read the column with parallel construction.

LACKING PARALLEL CONSTRUCTION	HAVING PARALLEL CONSTRUCTION
I enjoy *sewing* and *to plan* wardrobes.	I enjoy **sewing** and **planning** wardrobes. (Both items start with *ing* words.)
It's important *to make* good grades as well as *having* fun.	It's important **to make** good grades as well as **to have** fun. (Both items start with *to* and a verb.)
She expected a man *to have* a good job, *to be* good-looking, and *who would* pamper her every whim.	She expected a man **to have** a good job, **to be** good-looking, and **to pamper** her every whim. (All three items start with *to* and a verb.)
His experience made him *sullen, bitter,* and *a cynic.*	His experience made him **sullen, bitter,** and **cynical.** (All three are words describing him.)
She asked me *whether I could take shorthand* and *my experience.*	She asked me **whether I could take shorthand** and **what experience I had had.** (Both items are dependent clauses.)

By hard work and *because I invested my savings* in the company, I won a promotion.	**By hard work** and **by investing my savings** in the company, I won a promotion. (Both start with prepositional phrases.)
She wanted a house with *seven rooms, a two-car garage,* and *it should be in a good location.*	She wanted a house with **seven rooms, a two-car garage,** and **a good location.** (All three are words that can be read smoothly after the preposition *with.*)

Here are examples of thesis statements (see pp. 193–195 for an explanation of thesis statements), which of course should always use parallel construction. Note how each item in the last column can be read smoothly after the main statement. Those in the first column cannot.

My summer job at a resort was worthwhile because it gave me
  1. money for college
  2. I hadn't had a full-time job before
  3. had time for recreation.
	My summer job at a resort was worthwhile because it gave me
	  1. **money** for college
	  2. **experience** in a full-time job
	  3. **time** for recreation.

A college student should not live at home because
  1. he needs to be independent
  2. friendships in a dorm
  3. waste time commuting.
	A college student should not live at home because
	  1. **he needs** to be independent
	  2. **he will make** more friends in a dorm
	  3. **he won't waste** time commuting.

EXERCISES

Most of these sentences lack parallel construction. Cross out the part that is not parallel and write the correction above.

□EXERCISE 1

1. I like staying up late at night and to sleep late in the morning.

2. She seldom spoke of her privation, loneliness, and how tired she had been during those years.

3. Each student was given his choice of writing a term paper, taking a written exam, or he could make an oral report.

4. I enjoy a book that has a great deal of adventure in it and not too long.

5. I was trying to decide whether to be a teacher, a nurse, or to take up medicine.

6. She wants a house near the city and having modern conveniences.

7. She spent the summer collecting shells on the beach, identifying them, and then she made an exhibit of them.

8. I had read the textbook, read the reference books, written the term paper, and I had studied for the exam.

9. After we had eaten our supper, we put water on the fire, washed the dishes, and we packed the car for an early morning start.

10. My instructor says I have too many run-together sentences, too many fragments, and that I can't spell.

□EXERCISE 2

1. The doctor advised him to eat and sleep regularly and plenty of fresh fruit and vegetables.

2. My dad is intelligent, has integrity, and with a good sense of humor.

3. The politician promised to give jobs to everyone, to lower the cost of living, and yet increasing the profits of the business man.

4. His job makes him cross and always finding fault.

5. Finding a place to live, making new friends, and a new job were difficult.

6. This has been a great day, with a bright sun, a gentle fall of snow, and not too cold.

7. The lecturer was dull, unintelligible, and talked too long.

8. Among the advantages of my new job are the short hours, the good salary, and the boss is pleasant.

9. She was not interested in dating, taking part in athletics, or sorority life.

10. When I arrived at her office, she asked me to sit down, my name, and my age.

□EXERCISE 3

1. I enjoy bird-watching, hiking, and love camping out.

2. I have learned to adapt myself to new environments and how to get along with other people.

3. The average person does not know how air conditioning operates nor its cost.

4. My small brother likes candy, popcorn, and chewing bubble gum.

5. She liked to play solos and performing before an audience.

6. This course will teach a person how to decorate a house, the colors, the fabrics, how to choose furniture, and the kind of rug.

7. He arrived in the ancient city of Damascus, threaded his way through the narrow streets, and was taking pictures of the ragged children.

8. His only interests were singing, dancing, and to play tennis.

9. The cat was meowing pitifully and scratched at the screen door.

10. He will learn to work with other people and the value of cooperation.

□EXERCISE 4

1. There are the chickens to feed, the cows to milk, and the horses should be curried.

2. My roommate is studying painting, wood carving, and how to make etchings.

3. If you want to create a beautiful room, it is more essential to have a knowledge of interior decoration than having a great deal of money.

4. We had a wonderful time swimming, fishing, golfing, and we also rode horseback.

5. The speaker was interesting, inspiring, and entertained the audience too.

6. The naturalist guide pointed out the great age of the giant sequoias and how they resist fire and disease.

7. Some critics have said that Hamlet's tragic flaws were indecision and being oversensitive.

8. I'm learning to read more rapidly, to improve my vocabulary, and I'm also reading better books.

9. He spoke with authority, illustrated his talk with personal incidents, and then he concluded with a poem.

10. The weather was cold, damp, and often raining.

□EXERCISE 5

1. She worked for the school bond issue, for the new zoning law, and promoted the new hospital bond issue too.

2. He bought a suit that has an extra pair of pants and with a vest.

3. With tact, kindness, and having understanding, one can usually help a disturbed child.

4. They chose a house in the country because they wanted to grow their own vegetables, to give their children a country environment, and to enjoy the quiet of rural life.

5. A coaching career offered him a good salary, enjoyable work, and he would have security.

6. I would not vote for him because he has evaded income tax, he is not interested in conservation, and because education bills have never had his support.

7. To be eligible for the honor society, a student must have good grades, faculty recommendations, and take part in several activities.

8. We were dissatisfied with our room because of inadequate lighting, and there was too much noise.

9. We couldn't interest the homesick child in swimming, boating, or even to go for a hike.

10. He had worked as a farmhand, day laborer, chauffeur, and in a mine.

□EXERCISE 6

1. We tried to teach our puppy to sit up, to beg, and come when called.

2. I finished studying, had a snack, and then I went to bed.

3. The box is six inches long and five inches in width.

4. The couple went to Grand Canyon for a vacation and to paint.

5. I want a doctor who specializes in diagnosis and with a great deal of experience.

6. We were taught how to make a thesis statement and how to write clear paragraphs.

7. The city allows them to present their opinions, to make suggestions, but not the privilege of voting.

8. Her study contained an old roll-top desk, a typing table, and in one corner was her bulging file cabinet.

9. They chose a shag carpet that had nicely blended colors and made of nylon.

10. That morning they pruned the trees, sprayed the entire yard, and even were doing a little weeding.

□EXERCISE 7

1. He washed the dishes, tidied the house, and was waiting for Sue to return.

2. His talk was about law enforcement, gun control laws, and that crime is increasing.

3. He had traveled by land, by sea, and air.

4. Everyone in the fraternity was either a good student or musical.

5. He was quiet but a likable guy.

6. By careful planning, by smart shopping, and cooking economy meals, she stayed within their budget.

7. My new dictionary has clear type, good derivations, easy pronunciation symbols, but mainly I like the interesting illustrations in the margins.

8. This course is a requirement but also worthwhile.

9. "Go back to Mississippi, go back to Alabama, go back to South Carolina, go back to Georgia, go back to Louisiana, go back to the slums and ghettos of our northern cities, knowing that somehow this situation can and will be changed."—Martin Luther King, Jr.

10. By then I had learned how to change the oil, how to check the battery, and the way to change a tire.

□EXERCISE 8

1. My reasons are that it's expensive, flashy, and I don't need it.

2. He suggested doing all the exercises and that we rewrite our essays.

3. She is a woman with infinite charm and who always says the tactful thing.

4. Your duties will be preparing breakfast, washing the dishes after each meal, and to clean the house on Saturday.

5. Before beginning to write a term paper, you should collect your material, make a thesis statement, and then you should organize your material according to your thesis.

6. She told me that she intended to take the chance and not to worry about her.

7. At camp we learned swimming, boating, fire making, and how to cook on an open fire.

8. We found out what each was interested in, about our families, and what courses we were taking.

9. To be courageous in the face of danger, to obey orders unquestioningly, and physical strength are three qualities of a good soldier.

10. I had no idea where to find the food, how she wanted the meal prepared, or the way her stove worked.

☐**EXERCISE 9**

1. Her rooms contained souvenirs of her travels—a small Buddha from Japan, a clay dish from Egypt, and she had brought a marble inlay from India.

2. I liked his easygoing way, his good humor, his generosity, and that he could be depended on.

3. Gore Vidal, in commenting on the Bicentennial Year, said, "I should think a year of mourning would be highly salutary—for our lost innocence, our eroding liberties, our vanishing resources, our ruined environment."

4. After she had practiced for weeks, after she had perfected each phrase, after she had looked forward to the program for so long, she gave a brilliant performance.

5. She taught her preschool child by reading to him, by teaching him songs, by giving him construction toys, and she took him on little neighborhood excursions.

6. I respected his brilliant mind, his devotion to research, and he was also a warm human friend.

7. Unlike many older people, Ursula kept her mind alive with reading, her thoughts sharp with writing, and her spirit alive with friendships.

8. For a good study center you need a large table, a good light, a dictionary, and it helps if you have some snacks nearby.

9. Her garden included evergreens, deciduous trees, bushes, and there were all kinds of flowers.

10. She hoed them, weeded them, pruned them, watered them, and sometimes she even sat and enjoyed them.

□EXERCISE 10

Make the parts of these thesis statements parallel:

1. Every college student should know how to type because
   1. some instructors require typed papers
   2. saves time
   3. get higher grades

2. Going home every weekend is unwise because
   1. I spend too much time on the bus
   2. I get behind in my college work
   3. expensive
   4. miss out on weekend activities at college

3. Commercial billboards along highways should be prohibited because
   1. they often cause accidents
   2. mar scenery

4. Learning to sew is valuable because
   1. sewing your own clothes saves money
   2. creative

5. My chief objectives in this course are
   1. to learn to spell
   2. to learn to write well-constructed sentences
   3. being able to write a clear composition

WRITING YOUR OWN SENTENCES

Write five sentences using parallel construction in each.

AVOIDING SHIFT IN TENSE

If you begin writing a paper in the past tense, don't shift now and then to the present; and if you begin in the present, don't shift to the past. In the following paragraph the writer starts in the present tense and then shifts to the past.

> In *The Old Man and the Sea* there are various conflicts. The Old Man has to fight not only the marlin and the sharks; he has to fight the doubts in his own mind. He wasn't sure that he still had the strength to subdue the giant marlin.

It should be all in the present tense:

> In *The Old Man and the Sea* there are various conflicts. The Old Man has to fight not only the marlin and the sharks; he has to fight the doubts in his own mind. He isn't sure that he still has the strength to subdue the giant marlin.

Or it could be all in the past:

> In *The Old Man and the Sea* there were various conflicts. The Old Man had to fight not only the marlin and the sharks; he had to fight the doubts in his own mind. He wasn't sure that he still had the strength to subdue the giant marlin.

EXERCISES

In these sentences and paragraphs from student compositions there are shifts in tense, either from past to present or from present to past. Change the verbs in each example to agree with the first verb used. Cross out the incorrect verb and write the correct one above it.

□EXERCISE 1

1. In my excitement I stumbled over rocks and dirt and then finally I see what looks like a path.

2. Suddenly a cop stepped up to me and says I'd better move along.

3. He opens the door stealthily and then walked swiftly through the hall.

4. She looked at him quickly and then says, "You're not telling the truth."

5. I am walking along casually. Suddenly I stopped short at what I saw.

6. First he flunks two courses; then he dropped out of college altogether.

7. He asks me to work on the membership committee next year, and then he told me that committee never does anything anyway.

8. He looked straight at me and says, "Beat it."

9. He stopped me and says, "Which way to Camden?"

10. He gives us no instructions for doing the experiment and then was critical of our work.

□EXERCISE 2

1. The heroine is rescued immediately after the speedboat turned over.

2. I give a shout, and the others stopped and waited for me.

3. I saw a meadowlark in front of me, and I walk cautiously forward.

4. We start a big bonfire, and then everyone came to join us.

5. I worked almost all night on that paper, but when I read it in the morning, I'm far from satisfied with it.

6. It was one of the best things that ever happen to me.

7. We asked how the ticket sale was going, and we are told it isn't going at all.

8. Each student chose a topic and then gives his report before the class.

9. We sat there in the pouring rain and watch our team go down in defeat.

10. The book contained a description of how to prepare a garden for planting, and then it tells what flowers to plant.

□EXERCISE 3

1. My roommate and I would get along better if I don't play my stereo so much and don't come home late.

2. I give him all kinds of help, and then he said I never helped him.

3. The bad guy shoots at the good guy, but of course the good guy escaped.

4. I got all the ingredients for the cake ready and then discover that I haven't any eggs.

5. I kept hoping for a letter, but none ever comes.

6. She walked down to the beach to gather shells, but footprints show that someone else is down there too.

7. She sees a figure walking along the shore in front of her; therefore she turned and walked in the other direction.

8. We watched television every evening until someone comes in and turns it off.

9. Friends are important to me, especially because I had no close relatives.

10. She loved that little house where she had been born and goes back to see it again and again.

□EXERCISE 4

1. In the short story "The Secret Life of Walter Mitty," Mr. Mitty is first driving his car, but then in his mind the car became an airplane.

2. When Mr. Mitty's wife asks him why he isn't wearing his gloves, he suddenly thought of surgeon's gloves and became a doctor performing an operation on a millionaire banker.

3. I promised myself that I was going to study, but suddenly I fall asleep.

4. When I gave a shout, he hears me and comes running.

5. Her parents give her everything she asks for, but she was never grateful.

6. I heard a knock, and then in comes my old high school friend.

7. We pull and push and tug, but we couldn't move the barrel.

8. He tells us he'll write, but he never wrote.

9. During all that time we keep hoping we'll get a letter, and then finally he walked in the door.

10. She cleared off her desk, put away her typewriter, and then sits back to wait for her interviewer.

□EXERCISE 5

1. He looked at me and says, "I'm resigning."

2. I walked through the woods watching for rare birds, and then I spy a deer.

3. When I got into the city, I can't get my bearings and drove for blocks not knowing where I was going.

4. Every turn I took is the wrong one, and I get farther and farther from where I wanted to go.

5. Eventually a policeman stopped me and says I'm on a one-way street.

6. I backed up, but I still have no idea how to get to my destination.

7. She opened the door and then realizes that she had left all the lights on.

8. I do all the work in the course, pass the exam, and still I got only a C̲.

9. She worked as a volunteer at the hospital for over a year and gets a lot of satisfaction from it.

10. They wandered along the shore until finally they spot a cove where they can look for shells.

□EXERCISE 6

1. The candidate gave his speech, answered questions, and then came down from the stage and goes around shaking hands with everyone.

2. We worked the entire summer at the camp, and then at the end the director surprises us with an extra week's pay because we had worked so well.

3. Robert Frost wrote about the New England countryside and its people, but he writes bits of philosophy too.

4. Frost was recognized as a poet in England long before he has any reputation in this country.

5. In his "The Death of the Hired Man" Frost describes an old man who came back to a farm where he had once worked, and he dies there.

6. She slams the book shut, turns on the TV, and decided to call it a day.

7. She went to law school, applied for jobs, and gets into one of the largest firms in New York City.

8. We rented a boat, went out on the lake, and watched the sunset before we come in for supper on the beach.

9. The book gave an account of Freud's work, but it doesn't tell much about his life.

10. Berne's book lists the games people play and told why they play them.

□EXERCISE 7

1. I was always getting into something, and my mother punishes me severely.

2. He comes right up to me and said I couldn't park there.

3. If you become aware of word roots, familiar words will take on new meaning, and unfamiliar words could often be understood even without a dictionary.

4. I take one look at the clock and ran for the bus.

5. In the story the heroine gives up her right to the fortune, but she got it finally anyway.

6. We had been looking for a street sign and then finally we see one ahead of us.

7. The forsythia are in full bloom now, but the Japanese quince had not come out yet.

8. I finished the dishes, set the table for morning, and crawl into bed at midnight.

9. I went to my room to dress, but suddenly remember that my clothes were all in the washer.

10. He knocked, and then he ask if he can come in.

□EXERCISE 8

1. I went back to my room and look out the window.

2. We hiked to the end of the trail, and then we come back.

3. It's a good play. It was about a boy overcoming a handicap.

4. Last night I went to the basketball game. My girl friend come with me.

5. I wanted to do my best in that course; I give it all I have.

6. Most of the time I keep a study schedule, but then sometimes I gave up and just sat and listened to my stereo.

7. She did all she could for him, and then she come home.

8. Nature meant a lot to me; I love being in the outdoors.

9. My best friend took a week off his job and come down here to see me.

10. The Grapes of Wrath is a work of art because it brought out many themes that can be applied to our lives today. It shows how environment affects people and how love in a family was important.

□EXERCISE 9

That summer I decided to buy a radio receiver with the money I had earned mowing lawns. I set it up in my bedroom, and then I spent an afternoon putting an antenna on the roof. My mother stands down there on the lawn hollering advice at me because she's afraid I'm going to fall off the roof. In spite of her I finally get it up, and then I went inside and connected the antenna to the receiver. Presto! I am listening to radios all over the world. Eventually I decide I want a ham radio operator's license too so I could transmit back to some of the stations I was hearing. I got the license all right, but being young and shy, I never did much talking. Mostly I just listen and work on my equipment. After a few months I tired of my new toy and never did any more with it. The important part was buying the equipment and achieving the capability to use it. The challenge of striving for the set was more fun than actually having it.

□EXERCISE 10

As I traveled down the highway, I signal to turn left. I start the turn, and all of a sudden I heard a braking noise that could be heard for miles. A man had tried to pass me and had not seen my signal, probably because of the glaring sunlight. The man stopped finally. Really not knowing what I was doing, I pull off the road. Then it hit me, a sick feeling that reached all parts of my body. I stop the truck and get out, stunned but relieved.

WRITING YOUR OWN PARAGRAPHS

1. Write a brief paragraph in past tense describing an accident you once had.
2. Now describe the same accident as if it is happening at this moment.

AVOIDING SHIFT IN PERSON

You may write a paper in

First person—*I, we*
Second person—*you*
Third person—*he, she, one, anyone, a person, they*

but do not shift from one group to another. You may shift from *one* to *he* because they are both in the third person group, but do not shift from one group to another. For example, if your paper is an *I* paper, stick with *I.* Don't let a *you* slip into the last paragraph.

Wrong: In making experiments in chemistry *one* should read the directions carefully. Otherwise *you* may have an explosion.

Right: In making experiments in chemistry *one* should read the directions carefully. Otherwise *one* may have an explosion.

Right: In making experiments in chemistry *you* should read the directions carefully. Otherwise *you* may have an explosion.

Wrong: Few *people* get as much enjoyment out of music as *they* could. *One* need not be an accomplished musician to get some fun out of playing an instrument. Nor do *you* need to be very far advanced before joining an amateur group of players.

Right: Few *people* get as much enjoyment out of music as *they* could. *One* need not be an accomplished musician to get some fun out of playing an instrument. Nor does *one* (or *he* or *she*) need to be very far advanced before joining an amateur group of players.

Too many *one*'s in a paper make it sound stilted. If you begin a sentence with *one,* it usually sounds more natural to use *he* in the rest of the sentence. For example, it sounds stilted to say

One should follow a study schedule if one wants to be efficient.

It's more natural to say

One should follow a study schedule if he wants to be efficient.

Since *one* and *he* are both in the third person group, you can shift between them as you wish.

Many people today write *he or she* and *him or her* in an attempt to show that they have no sex bias, but such writing is often awkward and wordy. Here is the way a sentence from one of the following exercises would sound written that way:

> One should never let himself or herself spell a word wrong even in a first draft, for if he or she does, he or she simply reinforces a bad habit.

No one talks that way, and it isn't necessary to write that way. In this book the universal pronouns *he* and *him* are used to mean both sexes.

The problem you are most likely to have is letting a *you* slip into your writing. Whenever you write *you*, look back to see whether your entire paper is a *you* paper. If not, get rid of the occasional *you*.

EXERCISES

In these sentences and paragraphs from student papers change the pronouns (and verbs when necessary) so that there will be no shift in person. Cross out the incorrect words and write the correct ones above.

□EXERCISE 1

1. All those who want to go on the field trip should get your equipment immediately.

2. He was just walking along the way one does when you aren't going anywhere in particular.

3. A person can have a good time at any social gathering if you enter into the spirit of it.

4. As a rule a person can get a job if you really try and are willing to take what you can get.

5. It is wise for the inexperienced swimmer to stay out of deep water and to swim only when you are sure a lifeguard is on duty.

6. If you want to improve your reading ability, one should read a great deal of easy material.

7. One has to study day by day if you want to feel secure at exam time.

8. I always enjoy myself more if no one says when you have to be in.

9. I work harder when I know an instructor really wants to help you.

10. If a person eats a balanced diet, you will be more likely to keep well.

□EXERCISE 2

1. If one is working his way through college, you don't have much time to waste.

2. If one doesn't get enough sleep at night, you won't be able to concentrate during the day.

3. You should not strive to possess things, for eventually they will possess you.

4. I was scared of meeting the guys on my floor; you really had to have guts to leave your room.

5. Our team went out onto the playing floor, and when the game was about to begin, you could see the fans watching us eagerly.

6. After we got our seat belts fastened, the plane took off, and you could see the little farms like a checkerboard below.

7. We had been on the plane for eighteen hours, and you get pretty tired of sitting that long.

8. One has to work out every day if you want to stay physically fit.

9. Anyone who wants to lose weight has to cut out sugar, and you have to stick to some rigid diet.

10. If one is going into medicine, you have to be good in chemistry.

☐**EXERCISE 3**

1. If parents expect their children to be unselfish, you have to set the example.

2. If one spends all his time on one course, he may get low grades in the others. You should learn to allot your time fairly evenly.

3. The student who has a poor vocabulary will have a difficult time in college. You can improve your vocabulary if you work at it.

4. One shouldn't shift from I to you when you are writing an essay.

5. If a student expects to get much out of college, you have to set up a study schedule and stick to it.

6. If one expects to be a success socially, you have to consider the feelings of others.

7. He worked ten hours a day, and you can't do that long without feeling the effects.

8. If a student goes home every weekend, you are sure to get behind in your work.

9. He spent all his time practicing basketball, and you naturally can't get good grades that way.

10. If one is going to Washington, you should get plenty of travel literature to read ahead of time.

☐**EXERCISE 4**

1. If one doesn't read in preparation for his trip, you may not see all the sights one is supposed to see in Washington.

2. One should read about the National Gallery even if you are not much interested in art.

3. In the Smithsonian Institution one can see Lindbergh's plane and many other exhibits you have heard about.

4. If one has the time, you should certainly not miss going to Williamsburg.

5. One could spend weeks there, and still you would not see it all.

6. If a person wants to write well, you should read great authors.

7. If you do all the exercises in this book, one should be able to get an A in the final grammar test.

8. If you want to prevent air pollution, one's car should have a tune-up twice a year.

9. Anyone can learn to paint his own room if you will just watch an experienced painter.

10. One should use a good grade of paint, and you should not try to get by with cheap brushes.

☐EXERCISE 5

1. Your brushes should be cleaned with paint thinner and washed with soap and water after each use if one expects them to last.

2. Everyone who is going on the trip should buy your ticket ahead of time.

3. A person can maintain his weight if you simply watch your diet.

4. Anyone looking for bargains can find them if you read the evening paper.

5. Anyone who does not have tags on his luggage is taking a chance of getting your luggage mixed up with someone else's.

6. One needs to get plenty of sleep before an exam if you want your mind to be clear.

7. I like the feeling that comes when you have reviewed thoroughly and feel ready for any exam.

8. I like being with a person who acts as if he enjoys being with you.

9. If one is carrying a full college load, you won't have much time for TV.

10. When we went out into the woods that morning, you could see deer tracks in the snow.

☐**EXERCISE 6**

1. As we looked down from the plane, you couldn't see anything but clouds.

2. If one intends to be a lawyer, you will need to write well.

3. If one has unruly children, it is probably because you have not trained them properly.

4. If one wants to learn to spell, the first thing you have to do is make up your mind that you really intend to work at it.

5. No one is so poor that you can't give something to the United Fund.

6. Anyone can learn to spell if you want to.

7. One can always write a good thesis statement if you just give it some thought.

8. His grades were low, but you can't expect high grades your first term.

9. One can improve his vocabulary if you simply decide to use the new words you learn.

10. One's grades are usually in proportion to the time you spend studying.

□EXERCISE 7

1. After we took off, you could see the houses getting smaller and smaller.

2. We used to fight a lot when we were kids, but as you grow up you become more friendly.

3. The extra games would give the player valuable experience because you learn the most in actual competition.

4. I'm learning to spell, but I find you really have to work at it.

5. One should never let himself spell a word wrong even in a first draft, for if you do, you simply reinforce a bad habit.

6. If you want to learn oil painting, one should really take lessons.

7. I like living in a dorm because it gives you a chance to make a lot of friends.

8. You should get some hard physical exercise every day if one wants to stay healthy.

9. I had studied until midnight, and after that your brain just doesn't function very well.

10. One needs to do a lot of rewriting if you want to learn to write.

□EXERCISE 8

1. I think being a stewardess would be exciting. My life wouldn't be just four walls and a kitchen. I'd be in different places at different times. The thing that amazes me is that you get paid to travel and do all these exciting things.

2. Children are so open to everything, especially at the preschool age. You can share so much with them, and they in turn share with you. Children bring joy into my life.

3. The elementary teacher will play a big role in developing the mind of the student. What we learn in this critical period will be imprinted on our minds forever.

4. More time should be spent finding out what your roommate thinks and what the guys on your floor think. People should get more involved in college life because your life should not be lived in a vacuum.

5. In high school I took a course called General Woods in which you made a piece of furniture. You did this on your own with a little help from the teacher. I made a coffee table, which my teacher encouraged me later to enter in a state contest.

□EXERCISE 9

1. I think one is a better person in the end after having a traumatic experience. If we have to work with someone to overcome such an experience, we get closer to that person. You become a better person for it.

2. One's life style changes greatly once he gets to a college dorm. You have to get used to living with forty other people.

3. Recreation may be merely reading a book, or it may be physical recreation. I enjoy the latter because I'm an active person. I feel that recreation makes better workers. If I have a good time on the weekend, I

feel obligated to perform better in school or on the job. Through recreation you feel fulfilled.

4. It seems that every time I turn around, I'm faced with a different situation. There's always something new to learn or do. I never have time to get bored. No day is ever lost because you never get in a rut at college.

5. Being president of the French Club in high school did a lot for me. Having to preside at meetings and to greet people gave me an opportunity to develop poise. You always gain confidence from such an experience.

□EXERCISE 10

A terminal patient who is suffering should have the right to determine her future. If she has only a few months to live, I would ask for a sufficient drug to put me to sleep painlessly. I don't think a person has the right to take another man's life. The only person who should ask for euthanasia is the patient. No person should take another person's life unless you're the Creator of that person.

WRITING YOUR OWN PARAGRAPHS

1. Write a brief paragraph telling someone how to develop good study habits. It will of course be a "you should" paragraph.
2. Then write the same paragraph to yourself—an "I should" paragraph.
3. Finally write the same paragraph using "a student should" and using the pronouns **one** or **he.**

GETTING RID OF WORDINESS

Good writing is concise writing, writing that uses no unnecessary words. Don't say something in ten words if you can say it just as well, or better, in five. "In this day and age" is not as effective as simply "today." "At the present time" should be "at present" or "now."

Another kind of wordiness comes from saying something twice. There is no need to say "in the month of July" or "seven A.M. in the morning" or "my personal opinion." July *is* a month, seven A.M. *is* the morning, and my opinion obviously *is* personal. All you need to say is "in July," "seven A.M.," and "my opinion." Below are more examples of wordiness.

WORDY WRITING	CONCISE WRITING
at that point in time	then
refer back	refer
repeat again	repeat
personally I think	I think
he was there in person	he was there
a person who is honest	an honest person
forty acres of land	forty acres
eleven P.M. at night	eleven P.M.
very unique	unique
three different kinds	three kinds
usual custom	custom
my father he	my father
field of sociology	sociology
brown in color	brown

EXERCISES

Cross out the unnecessary words, or rewrite the sentence to get rid of wordiness.

□EXERCISE 1

1. It is her brown suit that she looks best in.

2. I consider him to be a genius.

3. He is the person who was appointed to be class representative by the president of the class.

4. I woke up at four a.m. this morning.

5. As an actual fact I was equally as good in sports as my brother.

6. At the present time I am taking math and in addition also a course in physics.

7. The usual custom is to give everyone a free gift the first day a new store opens.

8. My brother he was small in size, but he had big ideas inside of his head.

9. You don't have to refer back to past history to see examples of bribery.

10. His future prospects are probably few in number.

□EXERCISE 2

1. Another one of the athletes threw the discus a distance of ten yards.

2. At six a.m. that morning we saw an absolutely perfect sunrise.

3. In this day and age we are surrounded on all sides with crime.

4. In the year of 1975 absolutely nothing was done to solve the problem.

5. The fact that a new innovation is being used in producing the product means that the end result should be better.

6. We decided at that point in time to move our office.

7. Owing to the fact that I had missed several classes, I was aware of the fact that I would fail.

8. We were considering the question as to whether we should charge admission.

9. The fact of the matter is that my father he really and truly loves football.

10. My girl friend she's a very unique person.

□EXERCISE 3

1. Many people will agree with this point, and many will disagree with it, seeing the other side.

2. The story was written so that it made me seem to feel a part of it.

3. It really seemed to me as if it had actually happened to me.

4. He had committed all kinds of illegal crimes, and yet he was allowed to go absolutely free.

5. This was the girl who had been chosen as the representative of the department by the department members.

6. It was decided by the members of the club that there should be a cleanup campaign to get rid of the excess garbage in the park.

7. I considered it to be a worthwhile project.

8. There are many people who never read a book from one end of the year to the other.

9. It is his tall height that makes him such a good basketball player.

10. The melons were large in size and sweet in taste.

□EXERCISE 4

1. His attitude was of a puzzling nature.

2. I am taking some money out of my account in order to buy my books.

3. The reason why I don't like that course is because I actually don't understand it.

4. After our lengthy hike that lasted over eight hours we were hungry for food.

5. He had tried several different sports. These sports included football, basketball, and hockey.

6. We discussed the subject of having certain floors that would be designated as quiet floors, where no radios or TVs could be played during the hours that were designated as study hours.

7. My mother she always gives me a lot of final instructions when I am going out of the door.

8. No person on earth ought to decide for another person what kind of career he should enter.

9. I was really astounded at the way she took over the charge of the house and the managing of the meals and looking after the children.

10. You must first work out a thesis statement, and then after you have done that, you need to find all kinds of specific details to put into your paper.

□EXERCISE 5

1. The last point that I will try to make in this paper is the idea that you should learn more at college than just what you learn from your courses.

2. The cake was in the shape of a square and had candles on it.

3. The architecture on our campus is usually considered by most people to be impressive.

4. Owing to the fact that I did not hand my paper in on time, I probably won't pass the course.

5. The fact is that I am actually tired of the course.

6. And in spite of the fact that I had reviewed thoroughly, I failed the exam.

7. What I had wanted was an A in that course.

8. The truth of the matter is that now I am not going to get an A.

9. I would like for you to consider the question of whether or not you will let your name stand as a candidate for vice-president of our club.

10. In the event that he does not come to the dinner, we will be short one hand at bridge.

□EXERCISE 6

1. He is a man who can be depended upon to do what he says he will do.

2. He was of the opinion that the Democrats would win.

3. The great percentage of students do not leave campus on weekends.

4. He did not take into consideration her past record.

5. The fact of the matter is that he really wanted to fire her.

6. The board had to face the question as to whether they would support the dean's action or not.

7. Because of the fact that I was younger than the other contestants, I felt inferior.

8. There are a number of people who are planning to take the alumni tour to England.

9. It was three a.m. in the morning when we finally arrived.

10. All of the three different kinds of shells that we found were very unique.

□EXERCISE 7

1. There were a lot of people there.

2. In the month of April there were ten people hurt in accidents in the city.

3. At the present time thousands of acres of land are under water along the river.

4. Personally I think something should be done to prevent flooding.

5. It's my opinion that no one seems to be working on the problem.

6. In this day and age I think we ought to refer back to our parents' days and see how much better off we are than people were in those days.

7. I repeat again that there are many people who do not appreciate the many good things about our day.

8. For example at the present time modern present-day medicine has increased man's life-span by a goodly number of years.

9. Finally the doctor arrived on the scene, but absolutely nothing could be done for her.

10. The plane circled around the airport for half an hour and then disappeared from view.

□EXERCISE 8

1. One solution is equally as good as the other.

2. My final conclusion is that I'm really and truly not interested in the job.

3. A total of ten players were suspended.

4. They shuttled back and forth between their country home and their city apartment.

5. A personal friend of mine has made a new invention.

6. I have tried to collect together all the information I will need, and I hope the end result will be satisfactory.

7. They carried him to his place of residence in an intoxicated condition.

8. There is no doubt but that our team will win.

9. He is a man who has worked hard all his life.

10. Math is a subject that bores me.

☐EXERCISE 9

1. I was unaware of the fact that she had arrived.

2. The fact that he had not planned his talk made it monotonous.

3. I grew up as a child in a common ordinary home.

4. In my personal opinion there is no doubt but that justice is too slow in this country of ours.

5. What I am trying to say is that in my opinion justice should be swift and sure.

6. The tale I am about to tell you is a tale which is unbelievable.

7. In the month of September everyone comes back to the campus.

8. The reason he left college was that he wanted some experience in the wide world of business.

9. The fact of the matter is that I have absolutely no time to finish my paper.

10. When I do get it finished, you may be sure that it will be the best paper that I can possibly write.

☐EXERCISE 10

Rewrite this paragraph from a university publication, cutting it to about one-third its length by getting rid of wordiness, and see how much more effective it will be.

One of the main problems of a student entering university is how to find his way around the twelve floors of the Library and how to use the materials. The students are confronted by rows of books, journals, complicated indexes, abstracts and ponderous reference works, and need help in finding the information they seek amid the mass of material. The Library staff recognizes its responsibility to help them utilize all this material. Orientation programs are given to all new students. Many faculty members bring their classes to a particular subject area or to the Government Publications for an orientation. Short printed handouts are available, such as special subject bibliographies, how to use periodical indexes or Psychological abstracts.

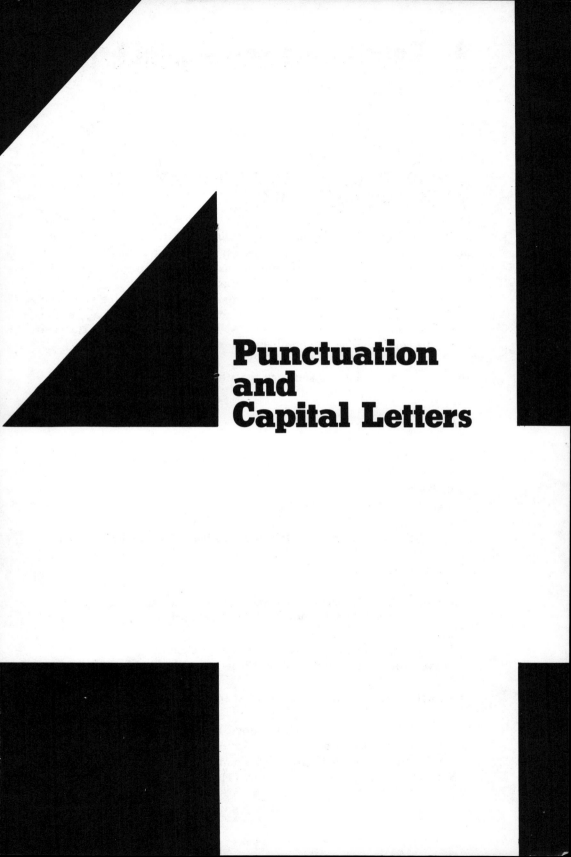

Punctuation
and
Capital Letters

4 Punctuation and Capital Letters

PERIOD, QUESTION MARK, EXCLAMATION MARK, SEMICOLON, COLON

Don't sprinkle your writing with punctuation marks as if you were shaking pepper out of a pepper shaker. Saying "I thought there should be a comma" or "There seemed to be a pause" is not a good reason for putting in a comma. Fewer commas are used today than formerly. Don't use any punctuation unless you know a reason for it.

Here are rules for five marks of punctuation. The first three you have known for a long time and have no trouble with. The one about the semicolon you learned when you studied independent clauses. The one about the colon may be less familiar.

Use a period at the end of a sentence and after an abbreviation.

Mr.	lbs.	Dr.	Wed.	sq. ft.
Mrs.	etc.	Jan.	P.M.	ibid.

Use a question mark after a direct question (but not after an indirect one).

Shall we go?
He asked whether we should go.

Use an exclamation mark after an expression that shows strong emotion.

Great! You're just in time!

Use a semicolon between two independent clauses unless they are joined by one of the connecting words and, but, for, or, nor, yet, so.

The rain came down in torrents; we ran for shelter.
I have work to do; therefore I must leave.

Use a colon after a complete statement when a list or long quotation follows.

We took the following items: hot dogs, fruit, and coffee. (*We took the following items* is a complete statement. You can hear your voice fall at the end of it. Therefore a colon is used before the list.)
We took hot dogs, fruit, and coffee. (Here *We took* is not a complete

statement; it needs the list to make it complete. Therefore since we don't want to separate the list from the first part of the sentence, no colon is used.)

EXERCISES

Add the necessary punctuation to these sentences (period, question mark, exclamation mark, semicolon, colon). Correct your answers, ten at a time, by using the perforated answer sheet in the back of the book.

□EXERCISE 1

1. Hurry We've only two minutes until takeoff time
2. We identified three new birds that day a golden-crowned kinglet, a field sparrow, and a hermit thrush
3. He asked whether we had seen her
4. Did he bring what you wanted from the city
5. We took her everything we thought a sick person might like books, flowers, fruit, and the latest magazines
6. Why don't you apply for the job
7. Hey I almost forgot that I've invited guests to dinner
8. What a stupid thing to do
9. Go away I want to work
10. You can reach him if you call before eight a m

□EXERCISE 2

1. Our candidate will be at the party therefore I want to go
2. The recipe calls for the following ingredients butter, milk, eggs, salt, and slices of bread
3. Why were you absent from class
4. The package was sent C O D
5. I asked him why he didn't come last night
6. Why don't you apply for the job
7. Hey I almost forgot I've invited guests to dinner
8. What a stupid thing to do
9. Will you sing for me
10. Why he hasn't come is a mystery to me

□EXERCISE 3

1. Why don't they stop this racket
2. He received his B A last June now he is working for his M A
3. A letter consists of the following parts heading, salutation, body, and conclusion

4. We walked through the deep woods to the creek then we sat down to watch the waterfowl
5. I'm taking English, American history, political science, and French
6. I'm taking the following subjects English, American history, political science, and French
7. What a commotion
8. What about Tommy Where's he
9. He asked why we had done nothing to stop the story
10. Why didn't you go with your brother

□EXERCISE 4

1. Not a trace of the old farm was left the buildings had all been leveled and corn planted where they once stood
2. They had no plans for the summer therefore we went to visit them
3. Why has it taken so long for him to get back
4. The cast includes the following students Craig, Stanley, Rita, and Kevin
5. The cast includes Craig, Stanley, Rita, and Kevin
6. The candidate's strong points are the following sincerity, adaptability, and dependability
7. Everyone was concerned everyone offered to help
8. At the auction she bought a sofa, two old chairs, and a popcorn popper
9. He asked whether he might join the party
10. The magazine contained stories, essays, and verse

□EXERCISE 5

1. Have you ever taken karate lessons
2. Their petition asked for three things shorter hours, double pay for overtime, and two-week summer vacations
3. I asked the policeman whether we could park inside the grounds
4. What do they expect us to do
5. He visited the following parks Yellowstone, Glacier, and Sequoia
6. He visited Yellowstone, Glacier, and Sequoia parks
7. How can you walk in all that wind
8. Look It's a sparrow hawk hanging in midair
9. Do you mean I'm supposed to sit here all day
10. I was awakened at four a m by shouts below my window I got up hurriedly and dressed

□EXERCISE 6

1. Stop You are ruining the picture
2. When the moon is fullest, it begins to wane when it is darkest, it begins to grow

3. She had all that money could buy home, servants, clothes, and cars
4. Help I've lost Archie
5. I studied until three a m then I went to bed
6. Isn't it about time he finished college
7. He wanted to know whether I had a scholarship
8. It takes two things to learn to spell determination and drill
9. He took the following courses in his freshman year English, economics, chemistry, and gym
10. The most famous English novelists of the nineteenth century are Dickens, Scott, and Thackeray

☐EXERCISE 7

1. We worked at party headquarters all morning then we canvassed all afternoon
2. The driver suddenly shifted gears then he stepped on the gas and was off in a cloud of dust
3. Does anyone have his car available
4. A person usually minimizes his own mistakes he magnifies those of others
5. They plan to visit the following countries New Zealand, Australia, and Japan
6. I worked a year after finishing high school therefore I won't graduate from college when my friends do
7. Who has left his books in my locker
8. I like the country roads with their sumac and bittersweet they remind me of my childhood
9. The snow was deep and crusty it was a perfect day for skiing
10. Wait I'm coming too

☐EXERCISE 8

1. He was correct that was exactly what I wanted to do
2. Couldn't he play, or didn't he want to play
3. The last race was about to start my confidence was building
4. Then came trouble in order to avoid a collision, I had to go over the starting line
5. Slam Unexpectedly a steel gate closed in front of me
6. He asked whether I had seen Ron
7. I finally found Ron he was in great spirits
8. This lesson includes the following punctuation marks period, question mark, exclamation mark, semicolon, and colon

9. Wonderful That's just what I need
10. The dainty Maryland yellowthroat warbled beside the stream

---

□EXERCISE 9

1. She asked me what I thought of Degas
2. During our days on the beach we picked up many kinds of shells conchs, cowries, limpets, oysters, and whelks
3. He had received his A B , his M A , and his Ph D before he was thirty
4. Did you phone me last night
5. Thornton Wilder wrote the following successful plays Our Town, The Skin of our Teeth, and The Long Christmas Dinner
6. They are going to the play, aren't they
7. Dan asked me if I intended to stay on the committee
8. A number of birds have visited my feeder all winter juncos, nuthatches, chickadees, and jays
9. I am interested in a number of career possibilities law, business, and teaching
10. Help Can anyone tell me how to start this paper

□EXERCISE 10

1. From nine a m to six p m I slept
2. Don't tell me what to do
3. "Quit it" he shouted
4. She sat there trying to decide whether to order chicken, lobster, or a steak
5. The fall quarter begins on September 5 and ends on November 28
6. The most unusual buildings in town are the courthouse, the old one-room schoolhouse, and the Thatcher residence
7. Hey Give me a hand
8. Her many duties included supervising personnel, reporting on projects, and attending board meetings
9. They asked whether they were intruding
10. The course was too difficult I soon gave up

WRITING YOUR OWN SENTENCES

On a separate sheet write three sentences using semicolons and three using colons.

COMMAS

Commas help the reader. Without commas a reader would often have to go back and reread to find out exactly what the author meant. The seven most important comma rules are given in the following sections. Master them, and your writing will be easier to read.

1. Use a comma between two independent clauses if they are connected by and, but, for, or, nor, yet, so.

We lost our oars, and that was the end of our boating.
We may leave Friday, or we may wait until Monday.
I wanted to go but could not get my car started.

The last example does not have two independent clauses (it has just one subject and two verbs); therefore no comma is needed.

2. Use a comma between items in a series.

Hurrah for the red, white, and blue.
She put down the phone, picked up her purse, and left.

Some words "go together" and don't need a comma between them even though they do make up a series.

The dear little old lady
The eager little boy
The dilapidated old building

The way to tell whether a comma is needed between two words in a series is to see whether *and* could be used naturally between them. It would sound all right to say *red and white and blue;* therefore commas are used. But it would not sound right to say *dear and little and old lady* or *eager and little boy;* therefore no commas are used. Simply use a comma where an *and* could be used. (It is permissible to omit the comma before the *and* connecting the last two members of a series, but more often it is used.)

3. Use a comma after every item in an address or date (if there is more than one item).

She lived at 251 Fifth Street, Canon City, Colorado, last year.
We visited Denver on our way to Palo Alto, California.
He was born on May 17, 1959, in Queen City, Missouri.

EXERCISES

Punctuate these sentences according to the first three comma rules. Correct each ten sentences before going on. Be tough on yourself. Don't allow yourself a single mistake, even though it was just a careless one.

☐EXERCISE 1

1. It was an exhausting futile task.
2. You'd better learn to rewrite or you'll never learn to write.
3. I write and write and rewrite but still my papers do not satisfy me.
4. Pipelines highways and canals have diverted much traffic from the railroads.
5. They traced him as far as Tucson Arizona and then they gave up.
6. The fidgety little old man amused everybody.
7. He was born in New York but moved to Los Angeles when he was five.
8. He had gone to an exclusive preparatory school.
9. England France and Russia were members of the Triple Alliance.
10. The greatest loss of life in the history of the world occurred in the earthquake in Shensi Province China on January 23 1556 when an estimated 830,000 people were killed.

☐EXERCISE 2

1. Her address was 4530 Evans Avenue Chicago Illinois.
2. She was intelligent charming and witty.
3. He is an eye ear nose and throat specialist.
4. You may write to him in care of American Express Buenos Aires Argentina.
5. Spinach is supposed to be healthful but I don't like it.
6. We made the lunch packed the car and laid out our clothes the night before.
7. He thinks he can predict the weather but he invariably fails.
8. The armistice after World War I was proclaimed on November 11 1918.
9. You can get the document by writing to the Superintendent of Documents Government Printing Office Washington D.C.
10. I've learned to avoid fragments run-together sentences and dangling modifiers.

☐EXERCISE 3

1. John Lees of Brighton England walked 2,976 miles from Los Angeles to New York City in 53 days 12 hours and 15 minutes.

2. He was looking for an investment that offered a chance of growth high interest and security.
3. Big billowy white clouds rolled in from the ocean.
4. Alaska was purchased from Russia on March 30 1867.
5. Many people want what they don't need and need what they don't want.
6. On April 8 1513 Ponce de Leon landed at St. Augustine Florida.
7. I looked in every store in town but I found nothing suitable.
8. From September 2 to September 6 1665 the Great Fire swept through London.
9. Jim hoped someone would come to relieve him for he had been there since morning.
10. He was too much interested in cars movies and television to do much studying.

□EXERCISE 4

1. On the plate were celery olives and radishes.
2. The three levels of government in the United States are local state and national.
3. She wore a black suit brown shoes and a green scarf.
4. The Stars and Stripes flag was adopted by the Continental Congress on June 14 1777.
5. He had worked hard but had gained little recognition.
6. I finished all my work cleared my desk and locked the office for the night.
7. I'm looking for an inexpensive black leather belt.
8. I had always been an eager conscientious student.
9. The Panama Canal was opened on August 15 1914.
10. We went back once more to that dear little old ramshackle cabin.

□EXERCISE 5

1. I have done my homework for tomorrow and I have also finished my term paper.
2. We were careful to mark our trail or Dick would never have found us.
3. Lincoln made his Gettysburg Address on November 19 1863.
4. The dull uninspiring lecture was finally over.
5. He slung his ice pick his oxygen mask and his knapsack onto his back.
6. We wanted to attend the lecture series but we couldn't get tickets.
7. It was difficult to support her husband her son and her parents on one hundred dollars a week.
8. The chairman appointed committees on decoration program and refreshments.

9. Our class reunion was set for ten o'clock on Saturday morning June 15.
10. The sky was full of soft gray clouds.

□EXERCISE 6

1. The sweet little old lady suddenly began to swear.
2. Walt Whitman was born near Huntington Long Island May 31 1819 and died on March 26 1892.
3. Could you meet me at Field's at noon on Tuesday March 3?
4. The office is located on the ninth floor of the Hart Building 540 Main Street.
5. The naughty little boy screamed louder and louder.
6. He had studied a great deal about the English American and French revolutions.
7. That beautiful old nineteenth-century house is being torn down.
8. The mean old bully annoyed everyone.
9. The three conifers in my yard are a blue spruce a cedar and a tamarack.
10. Although known as the chief interpreter of New England, Robert Frost was born in San Francisco California March 26 1875.

□EXERCISE 7

1. We couldn't do the decorating without a stepladder nor could we mow the lawn without a mower.
2. He put off writing his paper until an hour before class and of course did not get it finished.
3. No one really expected her to come but she was first there.
4. The political machine controlled the newspapers the courts and the police.
5. The letter, yellow with age, was dated January 3 1838.
6. The library displayed a number of manuscripts letters and notes written by Vachel Lindsay.
7. The crystal blue lake appeared before us.
8. Taxicabs limousines and trucks were tangled in a traffic jam.
9. The exhibit included water colors oils and etchings.
10. He couldn't decide whether to go into politics business or law.

□EXERCISE 8

1. Vachel Lindsay was born in Springfield Illinois on November 10 1879 and his home for many years was next door to the executive mansion.
2. She arranged the furniture hung the pictures and soon felt at home.
3. I used to drive a bright red Chevy but now I drive a little light blue Datsun.

4. A bore talks mostly in first person a gossip in third and a brilliant conversationalist in second.
5. Her mother was kind soft-spoken and devoted.
6. The child wore a tight blue cotton dress.
7. The child was surprised hurt and resentful.
8. He had done the best he could in the course but that was not good enough.
9. The fastest time for an around-the-world journey on commercial flights is 36 hours 19 minutes and 33 seconds.
10. You should spend more time on revising your essays or you will never learn to write.

□EXERCISE 9

1. We visited Mexico Guatemala and Panama last winter.
2. She was the first president of the Columbus Ohio chapter.
3. We stayed at Camp Alinet Devil's Lake Minnesota during one summer.
4. He was the handsome intelligent powerful leader of the opposing political party.
5. He won the local meet and he began practicing for the state.
6. We spent a delightful week at Turkey Run State Park in Indiana.
7. The prime minister's address is 10 Downing Street London England.
8. About the only date in history that he was sure of was July 4 1776.
9. We're leaving now for we're already late.
10. They lived at 631 East Ayer Ironwood Michigan until he was in high school.

□EXERCISE 10

1. We hoped to stop in Ogden Utah and Salt Lake City on our way home.
2. She had never mopped a floor in her life but she was willing to try.
3. Scandinavia is the ancient name of Sweden Norway Denmark and Iceland.
4. New York Chicago Philadelphia Detroit and Los Angeles are the largest cities in the United States.
5. An awkward ungainly figure stood at the door.
6. Every morning he had a breakfast of toast coffee and tropical fruit.
7. The road was narrow muddy and almost impassable in places.
8. She got out of the car slammed the door and went into the house.
9. The new owners of the farm had no interest in the past nor did they care anything about beauty.
10. The orchard the hedge and the hundred-year-old sycamores were all now a field of corn.

COMMAS (continued)

4. Use commas around the name of a person spoken to.

> Chris, how about a game of tennis?
> But I tell you, Mother, I must have the car.

5. Use commas around expressions that interrupt the flow of the sentence (such as however, moreover, finally, of course, I think, by the way, on the other hand, therefore, I am sure).

> I think, on the other hand, he may be right.
> He thought, however, that I should wait.
> We took our plates, therefore, and got in line.
> He asked, moreover, that we work overtime.
> I hope, of course, that they will come.

You can hear how these expressions interrupt the flow of the sentence. Sometimes, however, such expressions fit smoothly into the sentence and don't interrupt the flow; then they don't need commas around them. The expressions that were interrupters in the sentences above are not interrupters in the following sentences.

> However hard she tried, she could not please him.
> Therefore we took our plates and got in line.
> Of course I hope they will come.

You can hear that these expressions don't interrupt the flow of the sentence. Whether a word is an interrupter or not often depends on where it is placed in the sentence. If it is in the middle of the sentence, it is more likely to be an interrupter than if it is at the beginning or the end.

6. Use a comma after an introductory expression that doesn't flow into the sentence.

> Yes, I'll go.
> Well, that was the end of that.
> Running down the hill, she slipped and fell.
> When everyone had left, the auditorium was locked for the night.

When you studied dependent clauses, you learned that a dependent clause at the beginning of a sentence usually needs a comma after it. In the last example you can see that a comma is necessary. Otherwise the reader would read *When everyone had left the auditorium* . . . before realizing that that was not what the writer meant. A comma makes the reading easier.

EXERCISES

Add the necessary commas, using comma rules 4, 5, and 6. Correct each group of ten sentences before going on.

□EXERCISE 1

1. Because there were no important issues people were not much interested in the election.
2. We tried however to get everyone in our precinct to vote.
3. But however we tried we could not get everyone out.
4. Voters it seems are interested mainly in economic issues.
5. Taxation to be sure is a subject on which all voters should have a voice.
6. The entire country of course is concerned about the increase in crime.
7. What we need many think is stricter law enforcement.
8. Swifter and surer punishment they say is the solution.
9. Mr. Chairman I rise to a point of order.
10. Yes we'll be glad to help with the project.

□EXERCISE 2

1. Members of the Jury I have a moving story to tell.
2. I think most of the jury members were in sympathy with the witness.
3. Most of the jury members were I think in sympathy with the witness.
4. That company it seems had been guilty in the past of discriminatory hiring.
5. When I applied I had no difficulty getting a job.
6. After I finish college that is the company I want to work for.
7. Because many Americans are working shorter hours they are looking for something new and personally satisfying to do in their leisure hours.
8. Many are turning to home gardening especially vegetable gardening.
9. The zest for growing things it seems got a boost from climbing food prices.
10. Instead of watching TV many people are now tending their yards or gardens.

□EXERCISE 3

1. The program was on the whole quite entertaining.
2. Betty you should see that Egyptian exhibit.
3. No I hadn't heard.
4. Yes Warren there's a lot to be done.
5. However much you do it won't be enough.
6. It should not be imagined however that the task was an easy one.

7. As I've told you before Nancy I know nothing about it.
8. Yes we can take time for a break.
9. I'm sorry Madam that we do not have your size.
10. There are on the other hand great benefits to be enjoyed from such a career.

□EXERCISE 4

1. Of course we'll come.
2. Because he was so determined to succeed Clement worked far into the night on his studies.
3. Come on gang let's go.
4. We have of course given no thought to that question.
5. That was I think the last time I saw her.
6. I think for example that our present high taxes should be reduced.
7. Isn't it odd Ellen that he never even called?
8. After you have finished ten sentences check your work with the answers.
9. I'm hoping Jean that you'll come with us.
10. The car it seems was parked on the wrong side of the street.

□EXERCISE 5

1. We tried nevertheless to persuade him to go with us.
2. Your paper on the whole is greatly improved.
3. Yes it's much better I think than my first draft.
4. When I read my paper aloud I always catch some careless errors.
5. Since I have learned to write a thesis statement writing is easier.
6. Whenever I'm not sure of the spelling of a word I look it up in my dictionary before writing it even once.
7. Focused free writing I find helps me write more easily.
8. Even though I don't always like writing I enjoy having written.
9. While I'm in college I don't have much time for cooking.
10. I've been trying out a few new recipes however on my family.

□EXERCISE 6

1. He said moreover that he had no intention of finishing the job.
2. Our craftsman will I assure you mend the plate perfectly.
3. There's more room in this car Scott.
4. Come here Debra and help me hold this ladder.
5. Although we had a long way to go home we stayed until the end of the party.
6. Yes we seem to be making some progress.
7. When I really work my grades show it.

8. And we said furthermore that we would stand back of him in anything he chose to do.
9. He had despite his inexperience won the confidence of his peers.
10. Yes we have a big job before us.

□EXERCISE 7

1. Our football coach is I am sure the best anywhere.
2. You must not on the other hand be too particular.
3. Conductor will you stop at the next corner?
4. Sis you're wanted on the phone.
5. When a dependent clause comes first in a sentence put a comma after it.
6. It seems likely therefore that he will be asked to resign.
7. A man's character and his garden it has been said both reflect the amount of weeding done during the growing season.
8. I tell you Dale you're making a big mistake.
9. There are a few things nevertheless that he does not know.
10. Are you then the one responsible?

□EXERCISE 8

1. The speech on the contrary was quite ineffectual.
2. My interpretation of his speech is I believe unbiased.
3. The farmers it seems to me have had hard luck for a good many years.
4. I thought we might for example have place cards made of birchbark.
5. Well why shouldn't I enter the contest?
6. All right you may have it.
7. Well fellows the secret is out.
8. Remember Beth to bring my books with you.
9. Whenever I see crocuses I think of my childhood on the prairie.
10. The suit was to be sure rather large for me.

□EXERCISE 9

1. Of course I was glad to see her.
2. She was beyond a doubt the most unselfish person I ever knew.
3. You should I think improve rapidly now.
4. The party it seems to me should be financed from the surplus in the treasury.
5. You see Marie I didn't understand before.
6. Since I don't play bridge I get a lot of reading done.
7. Wouldn't it be better Dad to move the furniture before we start painting?

8. When I entered the door was wide open.
9. I was positive however that I had locked it.
10. The high grades you will find go to those who are most consistent in their work.

□EXERCISE 10

1. To improve your figure Sue you should take more exercise.
2. In the past I am told no inspection was necessary.
3. The evidence I suppose is contained in the letter.
4. She did as well as she could I think under the circumstances.
5. Who by the way is the chairman of the meeting?
6. When you are sure you have a good thesis statement then begin to write.
7. Of course I was happy to have them stay with me.
8. As I entered the door blew shut.
9. She was I think always concerned about me.
10. When I finished my paper was five pages long.

WRITING YOUR OWN SENTENCES

Write six sentences using the first six comma rules.

COMMAS (continued)

7. Use commas around nonessential material.

The material may be interesting, but the main idea of the sentence would be clear without it. In the following sentence

Gladys Nolan, who is heading the United Fund drive, broke her ankle.

the clause *who is heading the United Fund drive* is not essential to the main idea of the sentence. Without it we still know exactly who the sentence is about and exactly what she did: Gladys Nolan broke her ankle. Therefore the nonessential material is set off from the rest of the sentence by commas to show that it could be left out. But in the following sentence

The woman who is heading the United Fund drive broke her ankle.

the clause *who is heading the United Fund drive* is essential to the main idea of the sentence. Without it the sentence would read: The woman broke her ankle. We would have no idea which woman. The clause *who is heading the United Fund drive* is essential because it tells us which woman. It could not be left out of the sentence. Therefore commas are not used around it. In this sentence

The Grapes of Wrath, a novel by John Steinbeck, was a best seller.

the words *a novel by John Steinbeck* could be left out, and we would still know the exact meaning of the sentence: *The Grapes of Wrath* was a best seller. Therefore the nonessential material is set off from the rest of the sentence by commas to show that it could be left out. But in this sentence

John Steinbeck's novel *The Grapes of Wrath* was a best seller.

the title of the novel is essential. Without it the sentence would read: John Steinbeck's novel was a best seller. We would have no idea which of John Steinbeck's novels was a best seller. Therefore the title could not be left out, and commas are not used around it.

EXERCISES

Put commas around any nonessential material.

□EXERCISE 1

1. The fellow walking with the blond is my roommate.

2. My mother who bakes the best pies in town got a prize at the cooking exhibit.
3. The woman who got second prize is a friend of my mother.
4. The book that I was telling you about is now on the best-seller list.
5. Several of the books of Charles Dickens a nineteenth-century author have been made into movies.
6. The Satsuma vase I had brought from Japan stood on the mantle.
7. The adventures that he had during the summer were breathtaking.
8. The cat having lapped up its milk lay purring in the sun.
9. The night shift which did not end until midnight left him exhausted.
10. Sandy who thinks she looks like a movie star is taking dancing lessons.

☐EXERCISE 2

1. He went to his summer home which is in Wisconsin.
2. My brother trying out his new bicycle fell and broke his arm.
3. The boy riding a bicycle is my brother.
4. His home life which was remarkably placid was not the cause of his unhappiness.
5. The president's letter which had been missent finally reached Fred too late.
6. The boy carrying the flag led the parade.
7. The two longest rivers in the world are the Amazon flowing into the South Atlantic and the Nile flowing into the Mediterranean.
8. Lucien Smith my piano instructor is giving a recital tonight.
9. The dinner gong that she had brought from Egypt hung in the dining room.
10. My roommate who lives in Chicago usually gives me a ride home on weekends.

☐EXERCISE 3

1. Have you ever read I'm OK—You're OK a best seller by Thomas A. Harris?
2. On the next morning January 23 I went to work as usual.
3. The antique picture frame that she had resurrected from the basement now hung in her study as a showpiece.
4. Mr. Cox who is my favorite prof taught me how to read critically.
5. The company had hired an engineer who had had much more experience than I.
6. My client Mr. Hawk requests that the case be prepared for trial.
7. Her mother a very intelligent woman was successful in business.
8. The old man who was sitting beside me insisted on talking.

9. The rest of the passengers who were forced to listen must have been bored.
10. The house was filled with people who had come for the wedding.

□EXERCISE 4

1. Mrs. Janice James wife of a steel mill laborer ran for the senate.
2. Have you ever been in Minnesota the land of a thousand lakes?
3. Kilauea which was active when we were in Hawaii is one of the largest volcanoes in the world.
4. We have decided to get Eddie Gray's orchestra the best dance orchestra in the entire area.
5. She repainted the old chair that had belonged to her grandmother.
6. The car that has the red fenders is mine.
7. The Queen Mary which is now a Long Beach tourist attraction is a beautiful ship.
8. Bill who had almost fallen asleep jumped when the professor called on him.
9. Marcia who is the youngest in the group is always late.
10. The little cabin overlooking the river is ours.

□EXERCISE 5

1. This is the suit that I bought before Easter.
2. This suit which I bought before Easter is now too small for me.
3. More than a hundred years ago Hanson Gregory captain of a schooner and dabbler in the culinary art is said to have first put the hole in the doughnut.
4. The position that you told me about has been filled.
5. Don Johnson captain of the basketball team is ill.
6. The man who had been assigned to the job didn't report for work.
7. The Civil Aeronautics Board appointed to regulate the aviation industry has become a model for regulative governmental agencies.
8. No one who has studied Browning can fail to appreciate his poetic genius.
9. The motion that we adjourn was greeted with applause.
10. Maxie who is my best friend offered me his car.

□EXERCISE 6

1. Everyone liked our prom decorations which had sailing as a theme.
2. The boss sat down on the chair that was minus one leg.
3. My cousin Doris who is spending the winter in Florida is a landscape architect.

4. No one who knew him would believe all his stories.
5. Curtis Smith whom I had met only the day before asked me to the dance.
6. Just then in came Jamie a perfect godsend.
7. Pamela Sterling who is a member of the championship tennis team will attend the reception.
8. I am sure the man who lost his wallet will soon come back for it.
9. The hunchback of Notre Dame who was called Quasimodo the One-eyed grimaced at the assembled crowd.
10. Those who wish to have their term papers returned should sign the list on the front desk.

□EXERCISE 7

1. The midterm examination which will cover the information in the last five chapters will be given on October 15.
2. The girl who sprained her ankle was here this afternoon.
3. The photography contest which is open to all students will be judged by Dr. Bowen.
4. The anticlimax which had seriously weakened the plot of the book was omitted in the movie.
5. The city of Nassau is located on the island of New Providence which is twenty-one miles long.
6. Williamsburg which was at one time the capital of Virginia has been restored.
7. The place where Cabot landed is marked by a bronze plaque.
8. The hotel where the bandits sought shelter was the New Zealand Arms.
9. The book that was at the top of the best-seller list last week is in the library now.
10. The gift that I liked best was the little miniature horse.

□EXERCISE 8

1. Wayne who had grown up in a poor home finished high school at the head of his class.
2. The diet that I am following permits no sugar.
3. The apartment that I looked at first was too far from the university.
4. Living in the dormitory even with its disadvantages still is my best choice.
5. The woman hoped that the boy who had broken her window would pay for it.
6. All those who had worked in the political campaign felt rewarded by the outcome of the election.
7. The play that we saw last night was boring.

8. The boy who had the leading part exaggerated to such an extent that he was unbelievable.
9. Her grandmother's treadle sewing machine which had been in use for more than fifty years was one of her treasures.
10. The player who made the touchdown was sure of a scholarship for next year.

□EXERCISE 9

1. Walden which has become a classic was not a great success during Thoreau's lifetime.
2. Commas should not be used around expressions that are essential to the sentence.
3. This is the house that Jack built.
4. The largest and heaviest animal in the world and probably the biggest creature that has ever existed is the blue whale.
5. The town where my parents were born has a special place in my heart.
6. Arnold who used to be an English teacher now sails a boat.
7. I've done all the exercises that I was supposed to do.
8. Mike who is an authority on birds took me on a bird hike.
9. George Bernard Shaw who became one of England's most famous writers made only thirty dollars during his first nine years of writing.
10. James Thurber who was best known for his cartoons wrote humorous and satirical stories for The New Yorker.

□EXERCISE 10

1. Ulysses a novel by James Joyce describes the events of a single day in Dublin.
2. Ernest Hemingway author of A Farewell to Arms and For Whom the Bell Tolls was given the Nobel Prize in literature.
3. My cousin Pete who owns a farm near the city spends every weekend mending fences and cutting brush.
4. The Amos Place a quarter acre of unspoiled timber is a favorite nesting place for birds.
5. My older brother who has been studying agriculture is going to be a farmer.
6. Her living room which she had decorated herself was done in blue and ivory.
7. The living room that she had decorated was more attractive than the one shown in the magazine picture.
8. On her bed was a quilt that had been in the family for generations.
9. The team which had really worked hard all season was depressed by the defeat.

10. The authors whom we read last quarter were all from the nineteenth century.

WRITING YOUR OWN SENTENCES

Write six sentences, three of them having essential material and three having nonessential material. Be sure to punctuate them correctly.

QUOTATION MARKS

Put quotation marks around the exact words of a speaker (but not around an indirect quotation).

> He said, "I will go." (his exact words)
> He said, "Man is mortal." (his exact words)
> He said that he would go. (not his exact words)
> He said that man is mortal. (not his exact words)

Whenever *that* precedes the words of a speaker (as in the last two examples), it indicates that the words are not a direct quotation and should not have quotation marks around them.

If the speaker says more than one sentence, quotation marks are used only before and after his entire speech.

> He said, "I will go. It's no trouble. I'll be there at six."

The words telling who is speaking are set off with a comma, unless, of course, a question mark or exclamation mark is needed.

> "I will go," he said.
> "Do you want me to go?" he asked.
> "Come here!" he shouted.

Every quotation begins with a capital letter. But when a quotation is broken, the second part does not begin with a capital letter unless it is a new sentence.

> "A little learning," wrote Alexander Pope, "is a dangerous thing."
> "I object," he said. "We've worked hard. We deserve more."

Begin a new paragraph with each change of speaker.

> "May I have the car?" I asked.
> "What for?" Dad said.
> "To go see Kathy," I replied.

Put quotation marks around the name of a story, poem, essay, or other short work. For longer works such as books, newspapers, plays, or movies, use underlining, which means they would be italicized in print.

> We read Robert Frost's "The Road Not Taken."
> I read Margaret Mitchell's *Gone with the Wind*.
> I saw the movie *Animal Crackers*.
> Thurber's essay "Here Lies Miss Groby" may be found in his book *My World and Welcome to It*.

EXERCISES

Punctuate the quotations. If there are two sentences within a quotation, punctuate them properly. Also underline or put quotation marks around each title. Correct each group of ten sentences before going on.

□EXERCISE 1

1. Isn't it too stormy to walk she asked.

2. I'm too tired to go to the game he said I think I'll watch it on TV.

3. I hope you have enjoyed your work said the superintendent.

4. We haven't any red jackets said the clerk would you care to look at some other color.

5. One does not complain about water because it is wet, nor about rocks because they are hard said Abraham Maslow.

6. Nearly all men can stand adversity, but if you want to test a man's character, give him power said Lincoln.

7. Of war, George Bernard Shaw said that the men should all shoot their officers and go home.

8. Can't you wait for us she pleaded we won't be long.

9. No she declared I won't vote for him I won't vote for such a man!

10. The actions of some children said Will Rogers suggest that their parents embarked on the sea of matrimony without a paddle.

□EXERCISE 2

1. Alan Simpson gives this advice to young writers the first rule in English composition: every slaughtered syllable is a good deed.

2. La Rochefoucauld said as it is the mark of great minds to say many

things in a few words, so it is the mark of little minds to use many words to say nothing.

3. I won't be home until late she said because I'm going to canvass for the Heart Fund.

4. Doing work I like is more important to me than making a lot of money she said.

5. Hello he said how are you?

6. Do you really want to know how I am she asked.

7. A man is rich said Henry David Thoreau in proportion to the number of things he can afford to let alone.

8. Viewing the multitude of articles exposed for sale in the market place, Socrates remarked how many things there are that I do not want.

9. Snow and adolescence are the only problems that disappear if you ignore them long enough.

10. The best time to tackle a small problem said my father is before he grows up.

☐EXERCISE 3

1. Mark Twain said when I was a boy of fourteen, my father was so ignorant I could hardly stand to have the old man around. But when I got to be twenty-one, I was astonished at how much the old man had learned in seven years.

2. Mark Twain said the parts of the Bible which give me the most trouble are those I understand the best.

3. Work consists of whatever a body is obliged to do, and play consists of whatever a body is not obliged to do said Mark Twain.

4. I agree with the Spanish proverb how beautiful it is to do nothing and then rest afterward.

5. When Mom goes shopping said Kip she leaves no store unturned.

6. He found her munching chocolates and reading a book entitled Eat, Drink, and Be Buried.

7. Finish every day and be done with it said Ralph Waldo Emerson tomorrow is a new day.

8. Life can only be understood backward, but it must be lived forward said Kierkegaard.

9. George Bernard Shaw said few people think more than two or three times a year I have made an international reputation for myself by thinking once or twice a week.

10. The mind is everything said Buddha what you think you become.

□**EXERCISE 4**

1. I'm sorry, but I can't stay her visitor said because I must catch the 4:15 bus.

2. Why don't you help with the day care center she asked.

3. I would her friend replied but I already spend all of my spare time as a volunteer at the hospital.

4. Perhaps the most valuable result of all education said Thomas Huxley is the ability to make yourself do the thing you have to do, when it ought to be done, whether you like it or not.

5. James B. Conant, former president of Harvard, said that a liberal education is what remains after all you have learned has been forgotten.

6. Sometimes when fate kicks us and we finally land and look around, we find we have been kicked upstairs said Carl Sandburg.

7. Education does not mean teaching people to know what they do not know said John Ruskin it means teaching them to behave as they do not behave.

8. Let's go to McDonald's she said.

9. Do you want to go now or after the movie he asked.

10. Why not both times she said.

□ **EXERCISE 5**

1. The doctor asked can you read that chart in the corner.

2. Touchdown shouted the crowd.

3. Is this the street that Franklin Lacy lives on the woman asked.

4. No the boy replied he lives on the next street.

5. He said I'd go if I could.

6. He said he would go if he could.

7. I can't go he said I have to work.

8. A friend is a person with whom I may be sincere. Before him I may think aloud wrote Ralph Waldo Emerson.

9. Adlai Stevenson said with all its sham, drudgery, and broken dreams, it is still a beautiful world.

10. Napoleon once remarked the only conquests which are permanent, and leave no regrets, are our conquests over ourselves.

□EXERCISE 6

1. On observing the great number of civic statues, Cato, the Roman, remarked I would rather people would ask why there is not a statue of Cato, than why there is.

2. Nobody can carry three watermelons under one arm says a Spanish proverb.

3. The taller the bamboo grows the lower it bends a Japanese proverb says.

4. My father asked me why there was a dent in the rear fender.

5. I replied that I had not even seen it.

6. That's odd my father said.

7. We'll do our best to get the programs printed in time the printer said but we can't promise.

8. If we knew more said Herbert Spencer we would be more modest.

9. The Cathedral of St. John the Divine in New York City is one of the two largest cathedrals in the world said our guide.

10. Have you read The Telltale Heart or any other stories by Edgar Allan Poe?

□EXERCISE 7

1. Do you read Newsweek?

2. I have been reading Comfortable Words, a book about word origins by Bergan Evans.

3. All my spare time she said is spent in doing volunteer work at the YWCA.

4. Have you been back to the old school since we graduated he asked.

5. I've been back once she replied but nothing's the same.

6. You may have until Monday the instructor said to finish the assignment.

7. The best way out is always through said Robert Frost.

8. Henry David Thoreau said the cost of a thing is the amount of what I call life which is required to be exchanged for it immediately or in the long run.

9. William James said that the essence of genius is to know what to overlook.

10. Have you read Future Shock by Alvin Toffler?

□EXERCISE 8

1. The Secret Life of Walter Mitty is James Thurber's most popular short story.

2. The Catbird Seat is another popular story by Thurber.

3. Whatever you have you must either use or lose said Henry Ford.

4. Goethe said that men show their character in nothing more clearly than by what they think laughable.

5. The hottest places in Hell said Dante are reserved for those who in a period of moral crisis maintain their neutrality.

6. We went to see The Wild Duck, one of Ibsen's plays that is not presented very often.

7. At the end said Richard E. Byrd only two things really matter to a man, regardless of who he is; and they are the affection and understanding of his family.

8. The sword is always conquered by the spirit is one of Napoleon's most famous sayings.

9. Benjamin Franklin said dost thou love life then do not squander time, for that is the stuff life is made of.

10. The man who does not do more work than he's paid for said Abraham Lincoln isn't worth what he gets.

□EXERCISE 9

1. An art critic once said there are three kinds of people in the world: those who can't stand Picasso, those who can't stand Raphael, and those who've never heard of either of them.

2. John Gardner said that a span of time either leaves you better off or worse off. There is no neutral time.

3. Will Durant says that no man who is in a hurry is quite civilized.

4. Some people can stay longer in an hour than others can in a week said William Dean Howells.

5. After her weekend visitors left, she remarked guests always bring pleasure—if not in the coming, then in the going.

6. Henry David Thoreau, when asked if he had traveled much, replied I have traveled widely in Concord.

7. Sir James Jeans wrote there are at least as many stars as grains of sand upon all the seashores of the earth.

8. Our future as a nation is going to depend not so much on what happens in outer space as on what happens in inner space—the space between our ears.

9. Man's mind stretched to a new idea never goes back to its original dimensions said Oliver Wendell Holmes.

10. Are you coming she asked or shall I go on?

□EXERCISE 10

1. I can't always recognize fragments he said how can I be sure of them?

2. A fragment isn't finished she said it leaves you up in the air you are waiting for something more.

3. I guess I just need a lot more practice in picking out fragments he said.

4. Pablo Casals, the great cellist, spent hours on a single phrase. He said people say I play as easily as a bird sings. If they only knew how much effort their bird has put into his song.

5. Why aren't you writing your essay I asked.

6. Because I can't think of a thesis statement she replied.

7. Try some free writing I suggested and you may get an idea.

8. Harry Overstreet, writing in his book The Mature Mind, says to hate and to fear is to be psychologically ill.

9. Freud said that to have mental health a person has to be able to love and to work.

10. In the novel Fathers and Sons by Turgenev the main character says

that the chief thing is to be able to devote yourself.

WRITING YOUR OWN SENTENCES

Write a conversation that might be heard at your breakfast table any morning. Start a new paragraph with each change of speaker.

CAPITAL LETTERS

Capitalize

1. The first word of every sentence.

2. The first word of every direct quotation.

> He said, "This is the end."
> "This is the end," he said, "and I'll have no more to do with him."
>   (The *and* is not capitalized because it is not a new sentence.)
> "Why do you ask?" she said. "You know the answer." (*You* is capitalized because it begins a new sentence.)

3. The first, last, and every important word in a title. Don't capitalize short prepositions, short connecting words, or *a, an, the*.

> What a Property Owner Needs to Know
> What's the World Coming To?

4. Names of people, places, languages, races, and nationalities.

Grandfather Smith	England	Chicano
Uganda	English	Indian

5. Names of months, days of the week, and special days, but not the seasons.

February	Fourth of July	spring
Wednesday	Thanksgiving	summer
Labor Day	winter	fall

6. A title of relationship if it takes the place of the person's name, but not otherwise. If *my* is used before the word, a capital is not used.

Do you mind, Mother?	but	My mother doesn't mind.
I think Mother will come.	but	I think my mother will come.
I'm sorry, Grandfather.	but	My grandfather is seventy.
Come on, Sis.	but	My sister is coming.
I visited Aunt Martha.	but	I visited my aunt.

7. Names of particular people or things, but not general ones.

Call Dr. Simmons.	but	Call the doctor.
I spoke to Professor Olson.	but	I spoke to the professor.
We sailed on the Hudson River.	but	We sailed on the river.
I walked down Third Street.	but	I walked down the street.

He works in the Elks Building.	but	He works in that building.
The concert was in Browne Hall.	but	The concert was in the hall.
He went to Lee Community College.	but	He went to college.
I went to Macomb High School.	but	I was in high school last year.
Are you from the Middle West?	but	We turned west and then north.
I take History 301 and French 10.	but	I take history and French.

EXERCISES

Put in the necessary capital letters. Correct each ten sentences before continuing.

□EXERCISE 1

1. May I help you with the dinner, mother?
2. We discussed the matter with the professor.
3. He graduated from college and then went to spain.
4. All of the freshmen take history and english.
5. Margaret Mitchell gives a picture of the south in gone with the wind.
6. The detour took me south, then west, then north.
7. My aunt is the president of her club this fall.
8. Rich Fisher, the star of the basketball team, was honored by coach Hanson.
9. Lloyd Rudy is the president of a large steel company.
10. My sister is entering a ski tournament in the middle west.

□EXERCISE 2

1. The poem "in flanders fields" is often memorized in grade school.
2. He is classified as a freshman this year.
3. Are you going to take spanish or history as an elective?
4. He was selling time and ebony magazines.
5. The botany classes have been going on field trips.
6. You know, dad, I haven't had the car all week.
7. There is going to be a hockey game at the quincy rink tonight.
8. They called a doctor.
9. We went boating on the missouri river.
10. The colonial empires of britain and france are gone.

□EXERCISE 3

1. Usually college classes begin the day after labor day.
2. My grandfather took us boating on the river.

3. The football team was entertained by the Grand Forks rotary club.
4. A noted african explorer is going to speak to the high school assembly.
5. The doctor sent me to the hospital.
6. He enjoyed the fourth of july but paid up for it on the fifth.
7. Do you think everyone should go to college?
8. Fifty years ago the united kingdom ruled over one-fourth of the human race.
9. You have no idea, mom, what things are like today.
10. We visited Carmel, one of the most charming towns in the west.

□EXERCISE 4

1. The sun rises in the east and sets in the west.
2. I've lived on belmont avenue all my life.
3. While I was in high school I seldom studied, but college has changed all that.
4. He acts as if he lived on park avenue.
5. Last summer I went to a rock concert by three english musicians.
6. He decided to major in economics and minor in russian.
7. She spent the summer with her aunt in the east.
8. My father wants me to go to a state university, but I want to go to a junior college.
9. My uncle is president of the Canon City coal company.
10. The picture given in Rachel Carson's silent spring is coming true.

□EXERCISE 5

1. The fastest growing region in the world today is latin america.
2. Including mexico and central and south america, that area has grown from 86 million in 1925 to an estimated 319 million in 1974.
3. "Nothing matters now," she said, "except that you are here."
4. The university with the greatest enrollment in the world is the university of calcutta in india.
5. She graduated from a small high school and then went to Middlebury college.
6. I like Robert Frost's poem "stopping by woods on a snowy evening."
7. He had played before kings and presidents.
8. They went to a dance on valentine's day.
9. Next year I plan to take spanish, history, english, and physics.
10. I have professor Olson for french.

□EXERCISE 6

1. The John G. Shedd aquarium in grant park in Chicago is the largest aquarium in the world.

2. They all would congregate in front of the stores on main street on saturday nights.
3. It was a thrill to be on times square on new year's eve.
4. John Erskine wrote, "a beautiful woman is one I notice. a charming woman is one who notices me."
5. My high school friends have all gone away to other colleges.
6. "The tragedy of life," Thomas Carlyle said, "is not so much what men suffer but rather what they miss."
7. Hey, uncle Phil, may I borrow your car?
8. An Erie canal has no way of knowing how many ways a Mississippi river has of going wrong.
9. After he finished college he went to stanford university for graduate work.
10. She's from the middle west and has found it hard to adjust to the east.

□EXERCISE 7

1. He spent the evening reading how to win friends and influence people.
2. Hey, sis, whose bike do you have?
3. He resolved to speak no more arabic so that he would improve his english.
4. Mountain building occurred during the San Fernando earthquake in southern California in 1971, when within a few seconds some peaks of the San Gabriel mountains grew four feet as part of the San Fernando valley thrust itself under the mountains.
5. I'm hoping to go to the west coast this summer and from there to the yukon.
6. I spoke to my professor about dropping chemistry.
7. The headline read, "tougher meat laws needed in ontario."
8. "You don't understand," she said. "you've never understood."
9. Last year I took art 103, history 200, and a course in psychology.
10. My father went to the university of Chicago, and he's now a lawyer.

□EXERCISE 8

1. We visited yosemite national park and a lot of other state parks.
2. I thought, mom, that you would phone last night.
3. I went to the doctor's office in the gumbart building.
4. I had an appointment with Dr. McKendry, but another doctor saw me instead.
5. His office is in simpkins hall, but he teaches in browne hall.
6. Have you read games people play by Eric Berne?
7. She went to junior high school in williston, north dakota.
8. She graduated from waterville high school in kansas.

9. Anton Chekhov wrote many plays, the best known being <u>the cherry orchard.</u>
10. Mark Twain's most famous novel is <u>huckleberry finn.</u>

□EXERCISE 9

1. We traveled west that summer through the rockies and on to the west coast.
2. We were glad, though, to get back to the friendliness of the middle west.
3. We went swimming in the river every sunday when I was a boy.
4. We traveled east to Boston; there the difference in pronunciation of certain words left no doubt that we were in the east.
5. May I have the car, dad, or is mother going to use it?
6. My mother usually wants the car on thursday afternoons when she goes to Atchison women's club.
7. We spent some time at kings canyon national park.
8. Come on, sis, let's go.
9. My brother and I both attended galesburg high school, but we are going to different colleges.
10. "Five score years ago, a great american, in whose symbolic shadow we stand, signed the emancipation proclamation," said Martin Luther King.

□EXERCISE 10

1. He was in the vietnam war, but his brother fled the country because he did not believe in war.
2. My uncle often came to our house on summer evenings and told us stories.
3. Usually aunt Martha came with him.
4. I've signed up for history 201, math 200, english 101, and psychology 100.
5. I look forward to history and psychology but not to math and english.
6. He shouted, "what's happening?"
7. "Nothing's happening," she called back, "except that I've fallen off the ladder and broken my back."
8. I asked mother and father to visit me over thanksgiving vacation.
9. Have your mother and father ever visited you in the dorm?
10. They called for a doctor, and before long dr. Pex arrived.

Review Exercises for Punctuation and Capital Letters

Put in all the necessary punctuation marks and capital letters, and be ready to give a reason for each.

□EXERCISE 1

1. You'll find them where you left them son.
2. Psychology the class I like best comes at eight history comes at four.
3. I sent the letter to 413 Roosevelt Road Chicago but it came back unopened.
4. Emily Dickinson's terse brittle style in poetry has won her a large audience.
5. I sent my application to the university of california berkeley california.
6. When Max came up to visit me we went to see Sandra who is in the hospital.
7. We tried to be fair to him moreover we encouraged him to resign before his actions became known.
8. Lee Fraser the dean of our college is an understanding person.
9. Yes I'll do it for you she said when shall I begin.
10. His knapsack contained the following items food matches and a sleeping bag.

□EXERCISE 2

1. Severton hotel the old abandoned hotel on the south side of town burned last year.
2. He was hurt on April 20 1976 and he's been in the St. Francis hospital ever since.
3. I'm glad it's snowing now we can go skiing tomorrow.
4. Although I have not read Ghosts I have read a number of other plays by Ibsen.
5. Success is getting what you want happiness is wanting what you get.
6. It's hard for a fellow to keep a chip on his shoulder if you allow him to take a bow.
7. The trouble with the average family said Bill Vaughan is it has too much month left over at the end of the money.
8. Life said Samuel Butler is like playing a violin solo in public and learning the instrument as one goes on.
9. The lecturer spoke for over an hour but the audience did not grow restless.
10. Yes I suppose I am partial nevertheless I have tried to be fair.

□EXERCISE 3

1. My writing has improved greatly but I still have a way to go.

2. Since I have learned to write a thesis statement with supporting reasons I now find essay writing much easier.
3. Some people are affected by gloomy weather it has no effect on me.
4. I have three reasons for not going money time and lack of interest.
5. I decided moreover to cancel my subscription.
6. A little old lady from Boston refused to travel saying Why should I travel I'm here already.
7. Leal stated however that the committee was working on the problem.
8. Lend me a pencil Jeannette.
9. Two years later Milton left Cambridge and went to Horton a little village west of London.
10. Coming out of the capitol the senator said you save a billion here and a billion there and it soon mounts up.

□EXERCISE 4

1. No he didn't come we'll miss him.
2. An Arabian proverb says I had no shoes and complained until I met a man who had no feet.
3. You should see Berta's room mother it's decorated in tan blue and cerise.
4. Virgil Folsom my old school friend has gone to the university of New Hampshire to study.
5. What's wrong she asked.
6. He cried give me liberty or give me death.
7. Don't be frightened buddy.
8. The following men are on the affirmative side Harris Wilson and Boyer.
9. In 1973 man made his deepest penetration into the earth—11,391 feet— in Transvaal South Africa.
10. Are you going to town or are you going to study she asked.

□EXERCISE 5

1. Gandhi said Monotony is the law of nature Look at the monotonous manner in which the sun rises The monotony of necessary occupations is exhilarating and life-giving.
2. Can the story be true then that we read in the paper.
3. The Christian Science Monitor and The Wall Street Journal are excellent newspapers.
4. She spoke furthermore of our neglect of our duties.
5. I didn't study I went to a party instead.
6. Then I called on John Miller the local tailor.
7. Her attitude it seems to me is antagonistic.
8. I knew just what to say for I had been told what she would ask.

9. Students who do not have a <u>C</u> average cannot enter extracurricular activities.
10. The Taj Mahal which is in Agra is often called the most beautiful building in the world.

□EXERCISE 6

1. The gutters were full of water it was difficult to cross the street.
2. Figure skating which I am just learning takes hours of practice.
3. He plunged into the water and struck out for the other shore.
4. Full speed ahead ordered the captain.
5. As we put the horses in their stalls we could hear my father calling us.
6. The doctor at the clinic said he did not believe the report.
7. In the shop we found native handicraft drums grass skirts and tapa cloth.
8. Her house in Georgetown where I visited every summer was one place I felt I could return to.
9. Well what makes you think that.
10. All of these experiences had given Wordsworth a feeling of mingled appreciation reverence and love for the earth.

□EXERCISE 7

1. Kenneth she said your help has made all the difference.
2. He tried to improve his vocabulary by looking up new words by keeping word lists and by using the words in his conversation.
3. There is much inferior paint on the market but most consumer dissatisfaction arises from bad application.
4. William Butler Yeats who won the Nobel Prize in literature in 1923 was an irish poet.
5. There is much more to the story but I haven't time to tell you now.
6. The child fought bit kicked and screamed but his mother remained calm.
7. When I was in high school I memorized Robert Frost's poem the road not taken.
8. I've never had any experience but I think I could handle the job.
9. Our clock had stopped we almost missed the train.
10. Gretchen then moved to Houghton Michigan where she played in the Keweenaw symphony.

□EXERCISE 8

1. As soon as the snow was gone we spaded the ground and planted our seeds.
2. A girl whom I met at camp last summer is coming to visit me.

3. He wrote a noble generous letter to his old friend.
4. The highest speed ever achieved on land is 650 mph at Bonneville Salt Flats Utah on October 23 1970.
5. The embittered egotistical woman lived the life of a hermit.
6. Looking at television playing baseball and reading comics are my favorite pastimes.
7. Much could be done much has been done.
8. One of the girls got an A the rest got C's.
9. We followed the trail to the clearing then we turned south.
10. You know mom ten dollars doesn't go far these days.

□EXERCISE 9

1. Wheat corn and barley are widely grown in the United States.
2. We had finished our chores and we thought we deserved a break.
3. Hey wait a minute I need that book.
4. I need to do the following things improve my spelling get rid of wordiness and use more specific details in my essays.
5. I must not however neglect my other courses.
6. Allison one of the best students in the senior class has the lead in the play.
7. My mother who is not a writer herself is still a good critic.
8. Have you seen The Glass Menagerie by Tennessee Williams.
9. Ursula a young eighty-four-year-old shares with me her enjoyment of literature and living.
10. The sign in the dentist's office read support your dentist eat candy.

□EXERCISE 10

1. Dan one of my best friends is entering the university in the fall.
2. John D. Rockefeller, Jr., said that every right implies a responsibility every opportunity an obligation every possession a duty.
3. The Bastille fell on July 14 1789.
4. The three main forms of business organization are proprietorship partnership and corporation.
5. Lester is an unusually cooperative intelligent and helpful person.
6. Skiing skating and tobogganing were their chief winter sports.
7. Do you read Time or Newsweek.
8. I've changed my mind I'm not going.
9. Those were good suggestions Duane.
10. Helen who uses rare critical judgment in her typing does her work not only well but willingly.

Writing
Assignments

5 Writing Assignments

Assignment 1 Free Writing

"Writing is good for us," said Oliver Wendell Holmes, "because it brings our thoughts out into the open, as a boy turns his pockets inside out to see what is in them." Try "turning your pockets inside out" by writing as fast as you can for five minutes. Write anything that comes into your mind—no one is going to read what you write. Put your thoughts down as fast as they come. If you can't think of anything to write, just write words. Write anything, but keep writing for five minutes without stopping. Look at your watch and begin.

This free writing should limber up your mind and your pen. Try it at home. Besides helping you write more freely, it will help you sort out your ideas. Sometimes after you have discussed a problem on paper, it suddenly becomes less of a problem.

Now try another kind of free writing—focused free writing. Write for ten minutes as fast as you can and say anything that pops into your head, but this time stick to one subject—food. Look at your watch and begin.

Did you focus your thoughts on food for that long? Did you think not only of foods you like now but of foods you enjoyed as a child, of candy you bought with your first nickel, of foods your grandmother gave you, of foreign foods you have tried?

You didn't have time to include all those things of course. Once more write for ten minutes and add more to your discussion of food. Begin.

Focused free writing is a good way to begin writing a paper. When you are assigned a paper, write for ten minutes putting down all your thoughts on the subject. It will help you figure out what aspect of the subject to write about, and it will let you see what material you have.

As an out-of-class assignment, choose any subject that interests you and write for fifteen minutes without stopping. Time yourself. No one will read what you write.

Assignment 2 Getting Rid of Clichés

A cliché is an expression that has been used so often it has lost its originality and effectiveness. Whoever first said "light as a feather" had thought of a new original way to express lightness, but today that expression is outworn and boring. Most of us use an occasional cliché in

190

speaking, but clichés have no place in writing. The good writer thinks up fresh new ways to express his thoughts.

Here are a few clichés. Add some more to the list.

all work and no play	too funny for words
apple of his eye	work like a dog
as luck would have it	quick as a flash
as white as snow	sadder but wiser
better late than never	skin of our teeth
blue in the face	slowly but surely
bright and early	
by leaps and bounds	
center of attraction	
cool as a cucumber	
die laughing	
easier said than done	
few and far between	
heavy as lead	
last but not least	

One way to become aware of clichés so that you will not use them in your writing is to see how many you can purposely put into a paragraph. Write a paragraph describing your first morning on campus, using all the clichés possible while still keeping your account smooth and clear. You probably will start out something like this: "I was up at the crack of dawn, fresh as a daisy, and raring to go. First and foremost I wanted to . . ." It should be fun to write such an account, and it should make you so aware of clichés that they will never again creep into your writing.

Assignment 3 A Significant Incident

What incident in your life had a profound effect upon you? Perhaps it occurred in early childhood, in school, out of school. Write an account of the incident giving specific details so that your reader will relive it with you and feel its importance.

Here are two student papers on this assignment. Both students were having difficulties with spelling and sentence structure. At first their papers were so full of errors that they were almost impossible to read, but after a number of rewritings, they are now clear and understandable. These students had something interesting to say, and it was worth their while to get rid of errors in mechanics so that their writing can be read easily.

JASON

Two years ago at the District wrestling tournament, where I was wrestling with the team, halfway through the meet I noticed an apparently retarded boy talking to and annoying everyone. Some of the crowd moved to other seats. Everybody was watching and laughing, including the guys on the bench where my team was seated. I leaned over to the guy next to me, whom I've known for several years, and I said, "Ron, look at that weirdo up there." Ron then replied proudly, "He's my older brother Jason. He's a mongoloid." I felt like a real jackass!

Later when there was a break in the tournament, Ron's brother came down on the mat and attempted to wrestle like Ron does. Of course everyone was watching Jason in hysterical laughter. Ron then lovingly and proudly walked onto the mat, embraced Jason, and they walked off together. The whole gymnasium hushed, and a tear came into my eye.

THE DAY I STOOD AND BECAME A MAN

I reached the door of my home, sweating not from exhaustion but from fear. I opened the door. A calm feeling came over me as I sat down. One more day I had escaped. But no more would I run or hide. I would stand and be a man and fight. The next day as I walked to school, out from behind a tree the bully came. We stood toe to toe and eye to eye. Fear ran through my body. Then he swung and I swung. As blood ran from his nose, my fear turned to courage. But then something happened. The fight stopped. We stood toe to toe for a minute. No words were said, and then he smiled and I smiled.

If possible write your paper several days before it is due. Let it cool for a day. When you reread it, you will see ways to improve it. Put it away for another day, and again try to improve it. Then copy it in form to hand in.

Now you are ready for proofreading. **Read your paper aloud.** If you read silently, you are sure to miss some error you should catch. Read aloud slowly, pronouncing each word distinctly, so that you will catch omitted words, misspelled words, faulty punctuation, and so on. Make it a rule to read each of your papers **aloud** before handing it in.

When your paper is returned, correct all the errors, and put any misspelled words on your spelling list on page 291. Rewrite your paper completely if your instructor has given you suggestions for revising it. Rewriting is perhaps the best way to learn to write.

Assignment 4 Limiting Your Subject

Finding a subject is sometimes the hardest part of writing. For one thing, you need to limit your subject so that you can handle it in a 300–500-word paper. The subject "Food" was obviously too big. You might limit it by saying

My Dad's Outdoor Cooking
Food in Our Dorm
Cooking Chinese Food

but even those topics are too big. Keep making your topic smaller

Dad's Fabulous Sunday Suppers

and smaller

Dad's Specialty—Sloppy Joes

and smaller

The Day I Helped Dad Make Sloppy Joes

Now your topic is small enough that you can say all you want to say about it in 300–500 words.

Which of the following topics are small enough to be handled in a short paper?

Water Pollution	Pollution of the Creek Near My Home
My Hometown	The Drugstore Hangout in My Town
My Childhood	A Moment that Changed my Life
Illinois Is a Great State	The One-Room Schoolhouse in Macomb
Legalization of Marijuana	A Marijuana Incident in Our Dorm
Highway Billboards—A Menace	The Menace of Billboards at the Junction North of Town

Obviously the topics in the first column are too big; those in the second would be more manageable. Usually the more you limit your topic, the better your paper will be because you will then have room for specific details, which make any topic come alive.

List two topics you might at some time enjoy writing about, and be sure they are limited.

Assignment 5 Thesis Statement

Even after you have limited your subject, you are still not ready to write. You must first decide what point you are going to try to get across to your reader. The topic "The Day I Helped Dad Make Sloppy Joes" doesn't say anything. It doesn't go anywhere. It doesn't make any point. What about that day? What did it do to you? What point about that day would you like to get across to your reader? You might write

Helping Dad make Sloppy Joes made me want to learn to cook.

or

Helping Dad make Sloppy Joes gave me my first sense of achievement.

or

Helping Dad make Sloppy Joes made me feel closer to him than I ever had before.

Now you have said something. *When you write in one sentence the point you are going to try to get across to your reader,* you have written a **thesis statement.**

What was the thesis statement for the paper you wrote about a significant incident? If your paper was effective, you had a thesis statement in mind even if you were not aware of it. It would have been like one of these:

An experience at a wrestling match taught me not to laugh at the handicapped.
The day I fought a bully I gained new confidence in myself.

Write the thesis statement that you had in mind (or should have had in mind) when you wrote about your significant incident.

Now write thesis statements for the two limited topics you listed in the previous assignment. Each thesis statement—a sentence—will tell what point you hope to get across to your reader.

Assignment 6 Thesis Statement Backed with Supporting Reasons

Write in question form some problem or choice you are presently faced with. You might write

Should I leave home and move to an apartment?
Should I transfer to another college?
Should I change my major?
Should I drop out of college for a term and take a job?
Should I drop my girl friend/boy friend?
Should I go into _____ as a career?
Should I make fewer weekend trips home?

What you have written is a topic. Now write two thesis statements for your topic—one on each side of the question. You might write

I have decided to leave home and move into an apartment.
I have decided to continue living at home.

Each of these thesis statements tells the point you want to get across to your reader. Now they need to be backed up with supporting reasons. Put a *because* at the end of each thesis statement and list your reasons underneath it. You might write

I have decided to leave home and move into an apartment because

1. I need to become an individual rather than my parents' child.
2. I need to handle my own money.
3. I want to entertain my friends without parental supervision.

I have decided to continue living at home because

1. I don't have enough money to rent an apartment.
2. I like having my meals prepared and my washing done for me.
3. I like using the family car.

Three reasons usually work well, but you could have two or four.

Be sure your reasons are all in the same form. The above reasons all start with a subject and verb, and each one can be read smoothly after the *because* of the thesis statement:

because	I need to become. . . .
because	I need to handle. . . .
because	I want to entertain. . . .

If you write the reasons in different forms like this:

I have decided to leave home and move into an apartment because

1. I need to become an individual
2. handle my own money
3. no parental supervision

then you can't read the reasons smoothly after the *because* of the thesis statement:

because	I need to become. . . .
because	handle my own money. . . .
because	no parental supervision. . . .

If you read the last two reasons aloud, you can hear that they don't fit onto the thesis statement properly. Reasons don't have to start with a subject and verb so long as all three reasons start the same way. You could write

I want to leave home and move into an apartment because I'd like

1. to become an individual. . . .
2. to handle my own money. . . .
3. to entertain my friends. . . .

When all three reasons are in the same form, we say they are parallel. Be sure that the supporting reasons you write for any thesis statement are in parallel form. For a fuller explanation of parallel form, see page 111.

Perhaps the most important thing you can learn in this course is to write a good thesis statement. Most writing problems are not really writing problems but thinking problems. If you take enough time to think, you will be able to write a clear thesis statement, and if you have a good thesis statement, your paper will almost write itself.

Assignment 7 A Solution to a Problem

Write a paper on one of the two thesis statements you worked out in the last assignment. Even if your mind is not completely made up about the solution of your problem, take a stand on one side. You may mention that you can see arguments on the other side, but you must take a stand on one side if the paper is to be effective. No one wants to read a teeter-totter paper.

Your introductory paragraph should catch your reader's interest and suggest in some way your thesis statement. Usually it will not include the supporting reasons. It is more effective to let them unfold paragraph by paragraph rather than to give them all away in your introduction. (So that your instructor may refer to it, write your complete thesis statement with supporting reasons at the top of your paper above the title.) But even though your complete thesis statement does not appear in your paper, your reader will be perfectly aware of it if your paper is properly constructed.

Your second paragraph will present your first supporting reason—everything about it and nothing more. Be sure to use specific examples to prove your point. Don't just say, for instance, that you want to handle your own money. Tell how your parents have always handled your money for you in the past.

Your next paragraph will be about your second supporting reason—all about it and nothing more.

Your next paragraph will be about your third supporting reason. Thus each of your reasons will have its own paragraph. Keep everything concerning one reason in one paragraph, and don't let anything else creep in.

Finally you will need a short paragraph to sum up your conclusions.

It may even be just a single clincher sentence. One student, for example, wrote:

> Therefore I have decided for the above three reasons to pursue a career in veterinary medicine. And there is still another reason—my patients will never sue me for malpractice!

Your paper, then, will have five paragraphs:

> 1. Introduction arousing your reader's interest
> 2. Your first supporting reason
> 3. Your second supporting reason
> 4. Your third supporting reason
> 5. Conclusion

If you have two or four reasons rather than three, that of course will change the number of your paragraphs.

Assignment 8 A 100-Word Summary

A good way to learn to write concisely is to write 100-word summaries. Writing 100 words sounds easy, but actually it is not. Writing 200 or 300 or 500 words isn't too difficult, but crowding all the main ideas of an essay into 100 words is a time-consuming task—not to be undertaken the last hour before class. If you work at writing summaries conscientiously, you will improve your reading ability by learning to spot main ideas, and your writing ability by learning to construct a concise, clear, smooth paragraph. Furthermore, your skill will carry over into your reading and writing for other courses.

As you read the following essay, jot down any points that seem to you important enough to be put in a summary. Note that difficult words are defined in the margin.

THE RIGHT TO DIE
Bernard Bard

A father whose son was born a mongoloid raises the question of whether life should be preserved for such a child.

My son, Philip, was born at 11:20 A.M. on December 2, 1962, at Booth Memorial Hospital, Flushing, New York. The pediatrician, Dr. F., a youngish

Reprinted from *The Atlantic,* April 1968, by permission. Copyright 1968 by Bernard Bard.

man given to bow ties, met me in the corridor of
the maternity floor. It was a boy, five pounds, thirteen ounces, he said, but added: "I'm not totally
satisfied."

The vital organs were functioning normally, said
the doctor, but there was something about the facial features, the extra-wide bridge between the
eyes, the poor muscle tone, the weakness of the
stomach muscles when the infant cried that showed
abnormality.

"This is something we'll have to watch carefully,
to see how the baby develops in the next twenty-
four hours, or three to four days," said Dr. F. "But
for the moment, the outlook is for an individual
without a long life-span and not great mental development in the years ahead. Please call me by
tomorrow."

My wife was still under anesthesia. I went out to
buy flowers, and was in her room when she awakened. "How is the baby?" were her first words. I
said he was fine. She smiled and went back to
sleep.

I visited the nursery that afternoon and again
that night. My baby was in a warmer. The nurse
on duty assured me it was not an incubator, just a
temperature-control device. I had been worried
because Philip was premature, born four weeks
ahead of schedule. But the nurse told me his
weight was good. He looked beautiful. His face
seemed round and healthy-looking. I detected none
configurations—forms,   of the unusual facial configurations Dr. F. had
contours   mentioned. I began to grope for reassurance. I
stopped another nurse to ask how my son appeared
to her. "Fine," she said. "Don't let the warmer
worry you."

At three the next day, I sat in Dr. F.'s office, on a
residential side street a mile from the hospital. He
closed the door, and began, quietly, to recite some
of his observations. The ears were set back too far
on the head. The hands and feet were stubbier
than normal. There was an in-turning of the final
pinky—smallest finger   joint of the pinky fingers. There was a fold over
each eyelid. There was a scruff of fat at the back
of the neck. The hands and feet flexed back too far
under pressure, but did not reflex. "The child is

almost double-jointed." And the tongue was too large for the mouth.

The features and symptoms suggested hypertelorism, a word I immediately recognized as associated with mental retardation. The word for the infant's overall appearance and condition, said Dr. F., was mongolism. "All signs point to it." But still Dr. F. did not want to make his diagnosis final. He assured me tests could be taken, hip X rays and chromosome counts. And he could consult with the chief of pediatrics at the hospital. "How sure are you?" I asked. "Is there perhaps a fifty-fifty chance you are wrong?"

mongolism—type of mental deficiency accompanied with flattened forehead, slanting eyes, and so forth

No, said Dr. F., the odds were more likely ninety to ten that he as right. Few such children, he continued, live beyond the teens. Those that do survive into adulthood are incapable of reproduction. The outlook for "normal" mental development was about nil, he said, and only fifty-fifty that the child would be able to care for his own bodily functions, and not much more.

"Parents make either one of two decisions," said Dr. F. "Either they take the child home, and give him as much care as possible. Or, where there is another child at home, as in your case, the decision is sometimes made to institutionalize the mongolian child. Some parents take the child home for several months, or years, and then place it in a nursing home or training school."

That night I met Dr. L., the chief pediatrician at Booth. He emerged from the nursery, where he had just concluded his examination, and was still wearing his surgical mask and gown. "Wait till I shed this," he said. "I'll meet you in the father's waiting room."

There was no doubt at all about the diagnosis, said Dr. L. No tests were necessary. All the classic symptoms were present. The child, he said, would be vulnerable to heart trouble "of a severe sort," perhaps at age one or two. He would be peculiarly susceptible to digestive ailments and respiratory troubles. Life would, according to medical experience, be short. Mental development would be arrested at the age level of two or three.

classic—typical

vulnerable—open to attack

susceptible—liable

respiratory—relating to breathing

Dr. L. said many parents institutionalize mongolian children, "particularly when there is another child at home, a normal child." But he declined firmly to offer any advice.

Two days after Philip was born, I gave Peggy the entire story. Until then she had only known there were symptoms that troubled the doctors. She tried to nurse, but the baby was too weak. Dr. F ordered Philip be given a bottle in the nursery. I told my wife that I felt it best to have the baby cared for away from home, that this was a decision the doctors had not attempted to influence in any way, but one in which they concurred as the best. Dr. F. said, "He will grow up among children like himself, not aware that he is different."

concurred—agreed

In point of fact, the physicians I consulted said it was better to experience heartache now than to know a cumulative, greater anguish later on. To take the child home, one doctor said, would trap the family in "an irreversible situation." Peggy agreed, and said weakly: "Take me home."

cumulative—steadily increasing

irreversible—incapable of being undone

Through friends, I learned in the next few days of a private sanitarium in Westchester County, said to be rated one of the best in the state. I called and found my son could be accepted immediately. The institution, I was told, was run "as a hobby" by a pediatrician with a flourishing practice with normal children.

He was a specialist in mentally retarded children. The price, to families receiving welfare assistance, was $160 a month. I was one of these. My income, in the middle range, had forced me to apply to the Nassau County Department of Public Welfare for aid in meeting the costs of institutional care.

Now, among close friends, I began to tell our story. I learned that there are such tragedies in many families. The sister of a neighbor, I learned, cares at home for a mongolian boy of fifteen. He is virtually helpless, still wears diapers. The mother has suffered three miscarriages because of the strain of lifting him.

virtually—practically

A friend from my high school days told me of a cousin with mongolism, a woman of thirty-eight with the mind of a four-year-old. "I see her once in a while at a family social function," he said. "It's impossible to exchange more than a few words with her. Her mother's greatest fear is that she will be left alone, with no one to look after her, after the mother dies." The parents, I was told, were determined to have no more children for fear mongolism might strike again.

Another friend told of another mongolian child being raised at home. The mother has said openly: "I want to outlive him by just one day, so that I can know a single day of freedom." The child is in his teens. He often wanders away and gets lost in the neighborhood. The police bring him home.

On the weekend following Philip's birth, I visited the sanitarium which had been recommended to me. It was a large old mansion, constructed of brown and buff-colored stones. The premises looked solid, formidable, and cold; the design was turn-of-the-century; there was a small sign over the front entrance. The neighborhood was neat and partly residential.

formidable—causing dread

Mrs. C., the chief nurse, gave me the admissions forms. I paused, conscious of her watchful eyes, as I answered each question—father's name, mother's name, age of infant, weight, and so on. My feelings of guilt were overpowering. I felt I was abandoning my child. My mind returned to the hospital nursery. The other infants now there would come into homes made ready to receive them. My child was forsaken.

"Would you like to look around?" asked Mrs. C. We went first to a room containing the newborn. Nine infants were in cribs, some asleep. Most were awake. There was no whimper, no cry. The babies were almost motionless. They lay as if in a trance. Their faces showed no expressions. Most showed the telltale facial chracteristics of mongolism— eyes widely spaced, slight deformities of the ears, round, fat cheeks.

We passed down a corridor. Mrs. C. told me to wait while she closed a door. "The children in there have oversized heads," she said. "It might disturb you. We keep them together." On we went, into other rooms containing other children—mongoloids, brain-damaged; some were blind in addition to being mentally retarded. Some of the children seemed too large to be languishing helplessly in a crib; others seemed pitifully small.

languishing—lingering, lacking alertness

In one room was a girl of four, wearing a red playsuit. She lay on her back in the crib, staring blankly into space or at the ceiling. She was the age of my older son, Stephen, but half his size. "Mongolian," said Mrs. C. She affectionately tickled the child's stomach to bring on a playful mood. But there was no response, no laughter, no smile. The face was void. For my child, I told myself, there would be a crib here. It was a thought beyond total understanding or complete acceptance.

In her office, Mrs. C. listened as I told her of my feelings. It was not for this, I said, that we wanted another baby. We would consider ourselves blessed, I went on, if there had been a miscarriage or a blue baby rather than this. Mrs. C. understood. I asked her how mongoloid children fared. While they live, she said, "they haven't a care in the world—it's the parents who suffer." Heart failure kills many the first year, she said, but with new drugs more and more survive that period. If they do, she said, some mongoloid children live for years.

On the trip home, I prayed for my child's death, cursing and damning myself as I did.

I went back to see Dr. F., our pediatrician, who was pleased with the sanitarium and the speed with which arrangements were completed. I raised with him the question of euthanasia in those instances where neurological damage is so severe that no matter how long a child may live, he will be little more than a body—unable to care for the most elemental needs, totally dependent on others for survival.

euthanasia—painless putting to death of persons for reasons assumed to be merciful

neurological—relating to the nervous system

There was no shock on his face. Mongolism, said Dr. F., was incurable and the cause, usually, of gross retardation. If euthanasia were legal and professionally ethical, he said he would be more inclined to perform it on my child than on children afflicted with other diseases that were on the threshold of new discoveries. But for mongolism, he said, there was no cure and none on the horizon. Research was concentrating, he said, on birth defects so as to eliminate the prenatal causes of mongolism.

ethical—conforming to moral standards

While medicine could not take Philip's life, said Dr. F., nothing would be done to prolong it. No operations would be performed; no miracle drugs would be administered. "Medical emergencies will be met, such as sudden bleeding or choking," said

Dr. F., "and the child will be kept warm, fed, and sheltered. Nothing more."

I returned to the sanitarium in a day or two to meet Dr. K., the director. His offices were separated from the institution he ran by a narrow driveway. On one side of the driveway was the sanitarium, with its population of retarded children. On the other was a pediatrician's office, with baby carriages parked at the door. Cutouts of clowns and Humpty-Dumpties adorned the bright yellow walls of Dr. K.'s waiting room. There was laughter, and an occasional shriek, and mothers chased after children intent on mild havoc. At a small table, a group of children read aloud from a picture book.

havoc—destruction, disorder

Dr. K. is a man in his fifties. He has been a specialist in mental retardation among children for thirty years. He has examined every mongoloid child in Westchester County, it is said, either to confirm the diagnosis of other physicians or to contradict them. He spoke of mongolism in scientific terms, the papers he had written on it, the statistics compiled. Nothing, he said, had been discovered concerning precisely what goes wrong during pregnancy to cause the condition, marked by the presence of 47 chromosomes, one more than the normal human complement of 46. The research, he said, was attempting to find what body processes within the mother produce the extra chromosome.

complement—complete set

I told Dr. K. that I wanted nothing done to extend my son's hold on life artificially. He assured me he understood. The sanitarium, he said, contains no oxygen. The children are given no inoculations against childhood diseases, unless parents insist. "There are churches on all sides of me," he said. "Every one of these ministers agrees with me that it would not be moral, or serving God's will, to prolong these lives."

At the suggestion of an official in the welfare department, a social caseworker took Philip to the sanitarium next day. I had brought her diapers, nightgowns, blankets, bunting, and bottles for his formula. A few hours after Philip's arrival, Dr. K. called to tell me he had died. "Heart failure and jaundice," he said. 'Consider it a blessing." And I remembered what he had told me our first meeting: "Some parents regularly visit their children

jaundice—yellowish discoloration of the skin

expunge—erase   here. They waste their lives trying to expunge a feeling of guilt that should not be there, instead of devoting themselves to their normal children. It is for them that they must and should live."

I did not know my son. I do not know his thousands of brothers and sisters, of whom it has been written, "Oh, what a mortal pity he was ever born," and I do not know the parents of these children. I do not speak for them, just for myself and perhaps for Philip. I believe that it is time for a sane and civilized and humane approach to euthanasia.

I do not know how it should be practiced, or what committee should have a voice in the decisions, or what pill or injection might best be employed. I do know that there are thousands of children on this earth who should never have been born. Their lives are a blank. They do not play; they do not read; they do not grow; they do not live or love. Their life is without meaning to themselves, and an agony to their families.

Why?

Your aim in writing your summary should be to give someone who has not read the essay a clear idea of it.

If you have trouble deciding which points are most important, ask yourself what the author's purpose was in writing the essay. The important points, then, will be those that accomplish his purpose. You won't have room for details, and of course you won't include your opinion because you are writing a summary of the author's opinions only. Write as if you *are* the author, saying in a few words what he has said in pages. You will thus avoid such wasted expressions as "the author says." Generally you can write more briefly by putting ideas into your own words, but don't hesitate to use a phrase or sentence from the essay if you can't say it in fewer words. You need not put quotation marks around such quotations because you are writing as if you are the author.

Your first draft will probably be 200 words or more. Now cut it down by omitting all but the most important points and by getting rid of wordiness. Keep within the 100-word limit. You may have a few words less but not a single word more. And *every* word counts. You will force yourself to get to the very kernel of the author's thought and will gain a better understanding of the essay.

Make sure you have good transitions between points so that the entire summary reads smoothly. Use such transitional words as *also, thus, therefore, however.*

When you have written the best summary you can (it will take several hours), copy it to hand in. When you finish, **and not until then,** compare it with the summary on page 289. If you look at the model sooner, you will cheat yourself of the opportunity to learn to write summaries because once you read the model, it will be almost impossible not to make yours similar. So do your own thinking and writing, and *then* compare.

If you are not sure how yours compares with the model, ask yourself these questions:

Did I include as many important ideas?
Did I omit all unnecessary words and phrases?
Does my summary read as smoothly?
Would someone who had not read the essay get as clear an idea of it from my summary?

Practice writing summaries of material in other courses. Not only will such summary writing improve your reading and your writing, but it will help you master the material in any course.

Assignment 9   Thesis Statements on Euthanasia

Discuss, perhaps in small groups, the ideas in "The Right to Die." Consider these questions:

1. If you had been the author, would you have put your child in a sanitarium?
2. If it had been legal, would you have chosen euthanasia?
3. Is it ever permissible to take human life?
4. Should the law permit euthanasia for a severely abnormal child?
5. Should the law permit euthanasia for a person with a painful and incurable disease?

Many reasons will be given on each side of each question. As a group, work out a thesis statement with supporting reasons for each side of one or more questions.

Assignment 10   Getting Along with Someone

Write down the name of someone you have trouble getting along with. You may make up a name, but have a real person in mind. Write a thesis statement listing ways in which you wish that person would change so the two of you could get along better.

As we all know, however, it is pretty hard to get someone else to change. Therefore now prepare to write a thesis statement showing how *you* could change to make the relationship better. Perhaps you are thinking: "Impossible! There is no way I could change to improve the situation." Think! There are always ways.

Suppose, for example, you have an impossible roommate, someone who plays her stereo at all hours, comes in late and wakes you up, uses your toilet articles instead of buying her own, and so on. Obviously she is the one who should change. But your assignment for *this* paper is how *you* could change. Before reading any further, assume that you have such a roommate, and write down a thesis statement with supporting points showing how *you* could change to make living with such a roommate a bit easier. Don't say, "Impossible!" and don't write absurd suggestions. Think what you really could do. Write your thesis statement **before reading any further.**

You may have written something like this:

I could probably stand my roommate better if I would

1. suggest that we discuss our difficulties and try to compromise
2. spend more of my time at the library
3. think of her as an interesting specimen and try to figure out what makes her the way she is
4. work with others to get a floor of the dorm designated as a study floor

Now turn to the name you wrote down as someone you have difficulty getting along with. Write a thesis statement showing how *you* could change to get along with that person better.

As was said before, the problem in many papers is not so much poor writing as insufficient thinking. **Learning to write is learning to think.** Take time to think through your problem carefully; then write a good thesis statement; and after your instructor has approved it, write your paper.

Assignment 11 A Place Important to Me

What place means more to you than anywhere else in the world? A room? A house? A corner of a yard? A workshop? Write a thesis statement telling where your special place is and how it is important to you. You might write

A tiny spot in a ravine near our house was my refuge through childhood.
My room in our house in San Francisco is still a part of me.
My "hideout" under our porch was my secret place.
Our high school playing field is still important to me.

As you write your paper, try to make your reader understand how you feel about your place. What did it look like? Did you hear any sounds there? Were there any odors? Was taste involved? How did you feel when you were there? The more of the five senses you can make use of in your description, the more vivid your picture will be. Telling what happened in your place will also help your reader participate in your recollection.

Assignment 12 A Letter to a Parent

Most of us think our parents failed in some way, large or small, in bringing us up. Write a thesis statement telling what you think your parents (or one parent) did wrong. Then write another thesis statement telling what you think one or both of them did right. Choose one of these thesis statements and write a paper in the form of a letter to one or both of your parents.

Even though you are writing a letter, it will still be in the form of an essay—introduction, a paragraph for each supporting reason, and a conclusion. Your introduction might well be a brief statement of the other side of the question. That is, if you are writing about the things your parents did wrong, you might in your first paragraph mention that you know they did good things too and give a brief list. But the bulk of your paper must be on one side or the other. And remember . . . specific details make any paper come alive.

Assignment 13 Letter of Application

You may not need to do much writing in the career you have chosen, but almost certainly you will at some time need to write a letter of application. Write a letter of application now, either for a job this coming summer or for a job you might want to apply for after you finish college. Then on a separate sheet write a Résumé. Follow the forms given here.

500 West Adams Street
Macomb, Illinois 61455
February 1, 1977

Mr. John Blank, Director
Chicago Park District
425 East McFetridge Drive
Chicago, Illinois 60605

Dear Mr. Blank:

I have seen your ad in the Chicago <u>Tribune</u> for
helpers in the Park District Recreation Department
for the coming summer. I would like to be considered
for a position.

I am a freshman at Western Illinois University and am
majoring in Special Education. Therefore I would be
particularly pleased if I could work with mentally or
physically handicapped children.

I have listed my training and experience on the en-
closed Resume, and I shall be glad to come for an
interview at your convenience.

Sincerely,

John Doe

```
John Doe
500 West Adams
Macomb, Illinois 61455
Telephone: 000-000-0000
```

PERSONAL

Age 18
Height 5 feet, 6 inches
Weight 135 pounds
Unmarried

EDUCATION

1976-1977   Freshman at Western Illinois University. Majoring in Special Education.
1972-1976   Student at McKenzie High School, Chicago.

ACTIVITIES

Bowling
Swimming. Won second place in a swimming meet at Western in 1977.

WORK EXPERIENCE

1976 summer. Helper in County of St. Louis Department of Parks and Recreation. Worked with mentally handicapped children.
1975 summer. Worked at a private camp at Lake Minden, Wisconsin, coaching swimming.
1974 summer. Took a tour with a group from my high school to Washington, D.C., and then helped at the South Chicago YMCA pool, working with physically handicapped children.

REFERENCES

Mr. John Jones, Director
County of St. Louis
Department of Parks and Recreation
7900 Forsyth Boulevard, St. Louis, Missouri 63105

Mr. Henry Smith, Director
Lake Minden Camp for Boys
Lake Minden, Wisconsin 00000

Answers

6 Answers

Words Often Confused (p. 10)

EXERCISE 1

1. quite, dessert
2. They're, accept
3. Whose, course
4. led, past
5. advice, effect
6. peace, quiet
7. already, clothes
8. Does, weather
9. conscience
10. loose, lose

EXERCISE 2

1. whether, passed, course
2. You're, all ready
3. There, too, their
4. effect, advice, than
5. Whose, principles
6. compliments, clothes
7. quite, weather
8. You're, quiet, you're
9. does, loose
10. Their, affect

EXERCISE 3

1. an, course, a
2. quite, except, dessert
3. It's, fourth, already
4. forth, choose
5. too, too, weather
6. morale, personnel
7. accept, compliments
8. their, moral
9. advise, accept
10. You're, lose, accept

EXERCISE 4

1. dose
2. led, its
3. quite, advice
4. forth
5. led, its
6. an, past
7. It's, an
8. conscious, clothes
9. piece, loose
10. coarse, desert

EXERCISE 5

1. your, conscience, advice
2. It's, principles
3. They're, moral
4. loose, led
5. personnel, their
6. principal, passed
7. quite, too, to
8. lead, their
9. led, then
10. piece, advice

EXERCISE 6

1. Whose
2. affected, morale, personnel
3. morale
4. Does, they're
5. all ready
6. piece, coarse
7. an, effect
8. It's, choose, courses
9. advice, effect, than
10. whether, weather

EXERCISE 7

1. principal, too, compliments
2. Whose, advice
3. You're, clothes
4. accepted
5. choose, clothes
6. an, dessert
7. quite, weather
8. you're, too
9. their, than
10. choose, than

EXERCISE 8

1. Your, advice, already
2. an
3. fourth
4. chose, moral
5. their, past, already
6. your, course
7. Does, compliments
8. They're, than
9. weather, too, to
10. Desert, desert

EXERCISE 9

1. forth, peace
2. passed, dessert, fourth
3. lose, than
4. already, past
5. led, past
6. all ready, choose
7. Does, too
8. your, personal
9. than
10. already, two

EXERCISE 10

1. Who's
2. past, then
3. does, whether, you're
4. chose, desert
5. conscience, personal
6. Who's
7. It's, too, who's
8. principal, does
9. course, than
10. already

Doubling the Final Consonant (p. 16)

EXERCISE 1

1. putting
2. controlling
3. sweeping
4. mopping
5. turning
6. hopping
7. jumping
8. knitting
9. marking
10. creeping

EXERCISE 2

1. returning
2. swimming
3. singing
4. benefiting
5. loafing
6. nailing
7. omitting
8. occurring
9. shopping
10. interrupting

EXERCISE 3

1. beginning
2. spelling
3. preferring
4. fishing
5. hunting
6. excelling
7. wrapping
8. stopping
9. wedding
10. screaming

EXERCISE 4

1. feeling
2. motoring
3. turning
4. adding
5. subtracting
6. streaming
7. expelling
8. missing
9. getting
10. stressing

EXERCISE 5

1. forgetting
2. misspelling
3. fitting
4. planting
5. pinning
6. trusting
7. sipping
8. flopping
9. reaping
10. carting

EXERCISE 6

1. attending
2. compelling
3. napping
4. curling
5. amounting
6. obtaining
7. dreaming
8. crawling
9. cropping
10. descending

EXERCISE 7

1. permitting
2. despairing
3. eating
4. developing
5. quitting
6. exceeding
7. finishing
8. hitting
9. flinching
10. referring

EXERCISE 8

1. regarding
2. equipping
3. kicking
4. sitting
5. knocking
6. sleeping
7. skipping
8. leaping
9. shipping
10. mentioning

EXERCISE 9

1. stirring
2. mending
3. shrieking
4. murmuring
5. viewing
6. meeting
7. speaking
8. succeeding
9. pretending
10. deferring

EXERCISE 10

1. pulling
2. predicting
3. redeeming
4. patrolling
5. slanting
6. steaming
7. ripping
8. spending
9. tipping
10. tripping

Contractions (p. 22)

EXERCISE 1

1. Let's
2. Doesn't
3. Aren't
4. don't, it's
5. We're

6. I'm
7. Doesn't
8. can't, he's
9. Don't
10. You've, haven't

EXERCISE 2

1. It's
2.
3. don't, I'll
4. Who's
5. doesn't

6. doesn't
7.
8. It's, he's
9. You're, aren't
10. can't

EXERCISE 3

1. You'll, won't
2. Don't, I'm
3. can't, he's
4. Aren't
5. isn't, weren't

6. shouldn't, wouldn't, didn't
7.
8. can't, doesn't
9. couldn't, I'd
10. That's, wasn't

EXERCISE 4

1. won't, Won't
2. we're, shouldn't
3. Can't
4. wouldn't, hadn't
5. Don't

6. I'll
7.
8. What's, doesn't
9. That's, it's
10. Don't

EXERCISE 5

1. He's, hasn't
2. I'm, couldn't
3. Don't
4. I'm
5. I'm

6. I've, haven't
7. Haven't, They've
8. I'm, I'm
9. don't
10. can't, didn't

EXERCISE 6

1. I'm
2. You'd, you'd
3. Let's
4. Can't
5. That's

6. Won't
7. How's
8. Don't
9. I'm, I've
10. It's, she's

EXERCISE 7

1. It's
2. It's, can't
3. didn't
4. Can't
5. couldn't, didn't
6. We're, isn't
7. isn't, isn't
8. I'd
9. We'd, couldn't
10. didn't

EXERCISE 8

1. It's, weren't
2. I've
3. don't, we're
4. I'll, it's
5. I'm, you're
6. I'd
7. Two's, three's
8. Who's
9. wouldn't, didn't
10. He's, I've

EXERCISE 9

1. You're, she's
2. That's, I've
3. Isn't, she's
4. Don't
5. hasn't
6. We've, she's
7. She's, who's
8. isn't, you're
9. You'll, you've
10. They're

EXERCISE 10

1. She's
2. They'd, hadn't
3. I've, I'll
4. Wasn't, weren't
5. I'm, it's
6. We're
7. isn't, doesn't, it's
8. There's
9. It's
10. isn't, she's

Possessives (p. 28)

EXERCISE 1

1. girl's
2. ranger's
3. Ned's, Dennis'
4. men's
5. brother-in-law's
6. team's
7. Norma's
8. audience's
9.
10. team's

EXERCISE 2

1. chairperson's
2. Terry's
3. senator's
4. Jeffrey's
5. Someone's
6. Annette's
7. Yesterday's
8.
9. George's
10. night's

EXERCISE 3

1. Women's
2. world's
3. Dad's
4. Haley's
5. Lloyd's
6. Dad's
7. else's
8. brother's
9. Tom's
10. Charles'

EXERCISE 4

1. girl's
2.
3. wife's
4. father's
5.
6. Archibald's
7.
8. child's, parents'
9. Dickens'
10. Gerald's

EXERCISE 5

1. Chicago's, New York's
2. club's
3. Dylan's
4. college's
5. judge's
6.
7. Mr. Jones'
8.
9. Diana's
10. Nancy's

EXERCISE 6

1. Children's
2. Harry's
3.
4. anybody's
5.
6. dean's
7. day's
8. Saturday's
9. governor's
10.

EXERCISE 7

1. president's
2. Jerry's
3. Paul's
4. twins'
5.
6. dad's, mother's
7. Peter's
8. child's
9. dealer's
10. Ralph's

EXERCISE 8

1. settlers'
2. Ruth's
3. bartender's
4. Beethoven's
5. people's
6. Lincoln's
7. mother's, daughter's
8.
9.
10. else's

EXERCISE 9

1. Ted's, Tom's
2.
3.
4. students'
5. anybody's
6. everybody's
7. professor's
8. Someone's
9. mother's
10. Chaucer's

EXERCISE 10

1.
2. Johnsons'
3. father's
4.
5. Martha's, Sarah's
6. anyone's
7. Women's
8. James', Ervin's
9. Michael's
10. men's, boys'

Review Exercises for Contractions and Possessives (p. 32)

EXERCISE 1

1. She's, she'll, Faulkners'
2. Bert's
3. Shouldn't
4. Wouldn't
5.

6.
7. Won't
8. can't, didn't
9. We've
10. Carlyle's

EXERCISE 2

1. Clapton's
2. I'd
3. That's, what's
4. There's, Harold's
5. Dad's

6. Jim's, isn't
7. Can't, Janet's
8. couldn't, wouldn't, Becky's
9. Isn't, she's
10. wasn't

EXERCISE 3

1. It's, uncle's
2. didn't, else's
3. Hazel's
4. didn't, clerk's
5. won't, Saturday's

6. She's, mother's
7. hour's
8. We're
9. Didn't
10. I'm, we're

EXERCISE 4

1. Don't, it's
2. There's, students'
3. I'm, Ruth's
4. We're, Mr. Jones'
5. Here's

6. Gary's
7. I've
8.
9. Don't, Women's
10. I'm, won't, Vivian's

EXERCISE 5

1. Isn't, she's
2. Shouldn't, Francis'
3. It's, coach's
4. Mike's
5. Wouldn't, she'd

6. It's, I'm
7. children's, it's
8. Won't
9. dad's, mom's
10. women's, men's

Finding Subjects and Verbs (p. 38)

EXERCISE 1

1. grass is
2. He was
3. clouds covered
4. newspapers exaggerated
5. We sauntered
6. crowds moved
7. Night comes
8. attitude is
9. cities are
10. flames rose

EXERCISE 2

1. (You) stand
2. clouds rolled
3. halls are
4. instructor stressed
5. lizard darted
6. development was
7. exhibits were
8. Basketball requires
9. we saw
10. beds contained

EXERCISE 3

1. storm came
2. skiers wanted
3. deer was
4. sister broke
5. question was
6. we swam
7. book is
8. monument stands
9. Man is
10. We found

EXERCISE 4

1. I keep
2. (You) state
3. we stopped
4. They clambered
5. fire swept
6. motorist saw
7. he alerted
8. cabin burned
9. country needs
10. Jay dived

EXERCISE 5

1. jay took
2. chance was
3. water rushed
4. Fear spread
5. farmers made
6. others repaired
7. wave swept
8. sea was
9. They were
10. tapestry was

EXERCISE 6

1. he decided
2. (You) do
3. They went
4. reason is
5. glass quivered
6. face looked
7. He graduated
8. leader is
9. He is
10. boy came

EXERCISE 7

1. recipe calls
2. She received
3. strikers demanded
4. cedars were
5. speaker is
6. board included
7. Ted fell
8. We stopped
9. people reported
10. house contained

EXERCISE 8

1. work brings
2. galaxies are
3. I have
4. I recognize
5. papers make
6. I worked
7. trunk contained
8. We are
9. Aristotle was
10. Whitman rewrote

EXERCISE 9

1. person knows
2. odor rose
3. child stood
4. Dad gave
5. I had
6. I made
7. She liked
8. I exceeded
9. I trust
10. Juncos came

EXERCISE 10

1. plane soared
2. journey led
3. team fought
4. Swimming is
5. sound grew
6. man edged
7. Climbing requires
8. He carried
9. relatives live
10. wind swept

Compound Subjects and Verbs (p. 43)

EXERCISE 1

1. I went, walked
2. He wore, sported
3. I awoke, looked
4. we took, had
5. I wandered, picked
6. Magazines, books were
7. captain, crew escaped
8. King Arthur, court gathered
9. She stopped, waited
10. He majored, minored

EXERCISE 2

1. Swimming, tennis, badminton are
2. campers, guide hiked
3. thunder, lightning frightened
4. France, Spain are
5. Music, literature, art are
6. I brewed, carried
7. man took, drank, held
8. they filled, laid
9. They laughed, cried
10. She took, opened, found

EXERCISE 3

1. He visited, listened
2. president, dean conferred
3. incumbent, opponent engaged
4. I reached, smothered
5. She looked, saw
6. man shuffled, stopped
7. Lightning struck, split
8. wind howled, ripped
9. melody rose, died
10. amoeba is

EXERCISE 4

1. She was, offered
2. He, wife worked, settled
3. sister, I wash
4. *The Grapes of Wrath, Of Mice and Men* are
5. I rose, steadied, launched
6. boys joked, challenged, invited
7. captain walked, gave
8. He pruned, mowed, clipped, weeded
9. They searched, found
10. men mounted, rode

EXERCISE 5

1. She worked, saved
2. robins, meadowlarks are
3. Chemistry, physics were
4. rain, wind tore
5. friends are, are
6. Paper, pencils were
7. Bears, deer roamed
8. I expected, watched
9. class voted, appointed
10. I failed, had

EXERCISE 6

1. man opened, squinted
2. factories, commercialism came
3. He gave, asked
4. He, Ellen stopped
5. education broadens, deepens
6. child stood, caught
7. I wrote, began
8. I did, felt
9. peasants sow, string
10. Canadians, Americans fought

EXERCISE 7

1. She put, sat
2. He squared, began
3. House, Senate passed
4. I type, hand
5. maple, hemlock are
6. He dashed, clambered
7. I walked, identified
8. tragedy sobers, uplifts
9. Jackson, Swenson were
10. Jackrabbits, deer, chipmunks, squirrels, birds fled

EXERCISE 8

1. waxing, waning affect
2. Dr. Salk discovered, freed
3. Arabs marched, arrived
4. She devoted, saw
5. Queen Victoria ruled, left
6. Disraeli, Gladstone were
7. They deserved
8. Leonardo da Vinci designed, served, painted
9. They tugged, pulled
10. Music echoed, reechoed

EXERCISE 9

1. Jerry, I heard
2. History, math are
3. I sat, waited
4. She plays, sings
5. train choked, came
6. Essenes lived, held
7. swallows circled, darted
8. doctor, mate spoke
9. sand, sea, sky stretched
10. mountains, cliffs appeared

EXERCISE 10

1. boy leaned, whistled
2. mother, grandfather jumped
3. cabdriver pointed, shouted
4. Sartre, Camus were
5. time, money went
6. car careened, screeched
7. sun sank, disappeared
8. He made, followed
9. wind, rain drenched
10. mayor, owners opposed

More About Verbs (p. 49)

EXERCISE 1

1. You must have been working
2. Classes were dismissed
3. We have been going
4. Lincoln has been called
5. trees lose
6. men were imprisoned
7. She had seen
8. She did like
9. team had played
10. I have been working

EXERCISE 2

1. Everyone will be asked
2. players will be excused
3. Somebody will be held
4. books have been written
5. She does like
6. I have believed
7. I had eaten
8. pup has been tearing
9. He had been relying
10. He has been having

EXERCISE 3

1. singer was accompanied
2. I do like
3. game will be held
4. He was talking
5. She had been hoping
6. I have been having
7. He has been
8. He would have called
9. wife had been
10. You might offer

EXERCISE 4

1. They should have been asked
2. They have closed
3. I had been saving
4. She should have been doing
5. We have come
6. neighbors must have heard
7. You should have been told
8. They might have asked
9. I will have been working
10. I had been tutoring

EXERCISE 5

1. class had been studying
2. I should have told
3. words are divided
4. hyphen is used
5. heat had been
6. weather had reminded
7. matches were gleaming
8. cello had anticipated
9. stadium was rocked
10. farmers had been hoping

EXERCISE 6

1. Van Allen is known
2. lights are caused
3. Year was planned
4. cars could climb
5. flamingos were teetering
6. He could reveal
7. you can depend
8. I had been studying
9. power has become
10. He had been sleeping

EXERCISE 7

1. she had been collecting
2. She would identify
3. she would place
4. Limpets had been
5. shells could be found
6. Others could be found
7. They had been told
8. He had thought
9. They are waiting
10. France had acclaimed

EXERCISE 8

1. He had been concerned
2. mortar was used
3. designers are decreeing
4. He should have prepared
5. Shakespeare used
6. windows were produced
7. roommate plays
8. I can study
9. He has improved
10. She has been doing

EXERCISE 9

1. I have been working
2. bridge does look
3. She had been working
4. They thought
5. Van Gogh applied
6. Seurat would use
7. sound had broken
8. difficulties are caused
9. they saw
10. sun went

EXERCISE 10

1. I have liked
2. I had seen
3. She had been working
4. They had thought
5. They should have reported
6. team had been practicing
7. sound had ended
8. commotion was caused
9. they had seen
10. sun went

Subjects Not in Prepositional Phrases (p. 56)

EXERCISE 1

1. Many left
2. third studied
3. Most passed
4. we left
5. mountain rose
6. forest was
7. Both graduated
8. I am working
9. people crowded
10. we started

EXERCISE 2

1. fancy turns
2. Neither had been
3. she found
4. they ran
5. All have
6. I bumped
7. Some donated
8. she took
9. Millions read
10. Half bought

EXERCISE 3

1. picture is
2. One finished
3. Neither had been
4. top was
5. blackbird builds
6. we won
7. One disagreed
8. Neither likes
9. students posted
10. Each has

EXERCISE 4

1. One is
2. end was
3. all were
4. key was lost
5. Neither had been
6. Most eat
7. we saw
8. number is
9. members were
10. flight is

EXERCISE 5

1. Either will sign
2. Any may invite
3. Most would prefer
4. she won
5. composition will be
6. Most was spent
7. we discovered
8. Neither has
9. Most require
10. I phoned

EXERCISE 6

1. They gave
2. temples stand
3. All are held
4. One was
5. knowledge will help
6. Much is spent
7. he made
8. Everyone was annoyed
9. Men would have scoffed
10. age has encouraged

EXERCISE 7

1. Each was given
2. One was
3. we found
4. Most was spent
5. Two were

6. he had hidden
7. number had been placed
8. One is studying
9. room was filled
10. I learned

EXERCISE 8

1. faces grinned
2. we saw
3. we talked
4. result was
5. course had provided

6. sandpiper scuttled
7. waiter indicated
8. He stood
9. poppies grew
10. stagecoach jolted

EXERCISE 9

1. look settled
2. he yielded
3. America uses
4. product is
5. United Nations has received

6. it remains
7. Dissatisfaction is
8. Miriam has been
9. criminal slipped
10. letter is

EXERCISE 10

1. I must concentrate
2. end is
3. Picasso burned
4. book is
5. statue was reconstructed

6. glass has
7. forms can survive
8. He addressed
9. they licked
10. locusts swarmed

Run-Together Sentences (p. 63)

EXERCISE 1

1. arguments surprised, he had been
2. It does, (You) take
3. houses dotted, families were working
4. cabin was, firewood was
5. I do like, I can cook
6. boy ran, stopped
7. painting was finished, artist put
8. She is coming, she has
9. They're, they moved
10. Pronunciation changes, words are being added

EXERCISE 2

1. trees, house had shared, trees were being cut
2. (You) stay, it's
3. She can go, she is
4. She turned, light came
5. Wind began, night was
6. driver had been, he was hitting
7. It was, she was
8. He had made, he had had
9. TV was, people provided
10. door opened, child came

EXERCISE 3

1. wind blew, shutters rattled
2. We stopped, had
3. we did have, we could find
4. we found, it took
5. we had, wood was, it did burn
6. fire cooked, we found
7. I prefer
8. You can improve, it takes
9. He comes, he misses
10. You're, This can go

Only one punctuation is given for each sentence, but usually a period and capital letter could be used instead of a semicolon, and vice versa.

EXERCISE 4

1. moved;
2. you,
3. night;
4. class,
5. alarm,
6. country,
7. trotted;
8. face,
9. fellow;
10. fine,

EXERCISE 5

1. trout,
2. me;
3. skirt,
4. shove,
5. broke;
6. afternoon;
7. him? I
8. phone. It's
9. coat. It's
10. with? Will

EXERCISE 6

1. clear;
2. summer,
3. woods,
4. again,
5. untidy;

6. door. It's
7. tonight;
8. home;
9. worry. We'll
10. camp,

EXERCISE 7

1. plans;
2. forward;
3. days;
4. quiet;
5. torrents;

6. best,
7. in. Sit
8. aloud. You
9. her. You
10. himself,

EXERCISE 8

1. news,
2. you. Look
3. important;
4. times,
5. helpful;

6. go,
7. going? What
8. up. He
9. her. She
10. nature;

EXERCISE 9

1. blowing;
2. shore. We
3. door,
4. room. You
5. jeweler. He

6. cloudy. You
7.
8. work,
9. much,
10. us. We'll

EXERCISE 10

1.
2. interested,
3. world;
4. grandmother;
5. garden,

6. faithfully,
7. decorating. Her
8. tame. It
9. guitar. He
10. unpleasant;

Fragments (p. 72)

EXERCISE 1

1. S	6. F
2. F	7. F
3. F	8. F
4. S	9. S
5. F	10. S

EXERCISE 2

1. F	6. F
2. F	7. F
3. F	8. S
4. F	9. F
5. F	10. S

EXERCISE 3

1. S	6. F
2. S	7. F
3. S	8. F
4. S	9. S
5. F	10. F

EXERCISE 4

1. S	6. F
2. S	7. F
3. S	8. S
4. F	9. S
5. F	10. F

EXERCISE 5

1. When it grew too dark for reading, I watched my fellow passengers.

2. He took his van although he really preferred his motorcycle.

3. He was searching for the money that he had dropped in the snow.

4. The book is an account of the expedition of William Beebe to South America, where he set up his laboratory for the study of animal life.

5. When the sun went down, the air became cool.

6. As it became dark, we watched the stars.

7. As he dashed after each ball, he grew breathless.

8. Until you understand subjects and verbs, you cannot understand clauses.

9. She sprained her ankle last night while she was skiing.

10. The crowd roared with excitement as one of the Navy players raced down to the goal line.

EXERCISE 6

1. She chased the puppy through the house until she finally caught him.

2. I should have been waiting still if you had not called.

3. Unless you make an appointment, you cannot see him.

4. One does not do his best when he is tired.

5. This is the third time that I have told him.

6. While Angles, Saxons, and Jutes were still unknown Germanic tribes, their future island home was being made into a province of the Roman Empire.

7. I have always hoped that I could someday go to a Super Bowl championship game.

8. Although I studied hard, I still found the exam difficult.

9. *Oliver Twist* is a novel of poverty, crime, and injustice as they existed in the London of the nineteenth century.

10. I am not sure that I should go.

EXERCISE 7

1. that most often accompanies outstanding success
2. After I finish college
3. that were dropped during World War II
4.
5. that they are doing
6. because I had homework to do
7. if I studied
8. while he was studying
9. because I didn't have my textbook
10. Unless you return your library book today

EXERCISE 8

1. that gives me the most trouble
2. who is always punctual
3. that you cannot get from books
4. while the sun shines
5. that reason should control man's life
6. until his rescuers arrived
7. before they ate their lunch
8. while the Monty Python show was on
9. if she had rewritten it
10. Although he could never walk again

EXERCISE 9

1. that he needed
2. when our football team came onto the field
3. until the bell rings
4. that he was writing on the wrong topic
5. If you are too busy for a vacation
6. While she is away
7. When the fire siren sounds
8. If it is nice tomorrow
9. Although he hates grammar
10. Because the storm came up so suddenly

EXERCISE 10

1. Although it snowed yesterday
2. what he will say
3. When he was a child
4. which was homemade
5. While I waited
6. that he is telling the truth
7. that they received
8. Although we are the wealthiest member of the United Nations
9.
10. While the leaves were still on the trees

More about Fragments (p. 78)

EXERCISE 1

1. F		6. F	
2. F		7. S	
3. S		8. F	
4. F		9. F	
5. F		10. F	

EXERCISE 2

1. F		6. F	
2. F		7. S	
3. F		8. F	
4. F		9. S	
5. F		10. F	

EXERCISE 3

1. F		6. F	
2. F		7. F	
3. S		8. F	
4. S		9. F	
5. F		10. S	

EXERCISE 4

1. F		6. F	
2. F		7. F	
3. S		8. F	
4. F		9. F	
5. S		10. S	

EXERCISE 5

1. S		6. S	
2. F		7. F	
3. F		8. F	
4. F		9. F	
5. S		10. F	

EXERCISE 6

1. S		6. F	
2. S		7. F	
3. F		8. F	
4. F		9. F	
5. F		10. F	

EXERCISE 7

1. F	6. F
2. F	7. F
3. F	8. F
4. F	9. F
5. F	10. F

EXERCISE 8

1. F	6. F
2. S	7. S
3. F	8. S
4. F	9. F
5. F	10. F

EXERCISE 9

1. F	6. F
2. F	7. F
3. F	8. S
4. F	9. F
5. F	10. S

EXERCISE 10

1. F	6. F
2. S	7. F
3. F	8. S
4. S	9. F
5. F	10. F

Getting Rid of Misplaced or Dangling Modifiers (p. 86)

EXERCISE 1

1. Years later you will enjoy looking at the pictures you took.
2. I came across my grandfather sound asleep on the front porch.
3. I saw a furry little caterpillar crawling across the dusty road.
4. As he took her in his arms, the moon hid behind a cloud.
5. Thoughtfully beginning to dress, he was reminded by the new blue jeans and clean shirt that at last he had a job.
6.
7. Working really hard, I finished the term paper in six hours.
8. When I was ten years old, my mother gave me a ring.
9. After asking three or four people, we finally found the right road.
10. I was sure I saw an airplane crashing to the ground.

EXERCISE 2

1. After I had cleaned my room, my dog wanted to go for a walk.
2. After he graduated from grammar school, his mother took him to Europe.
3. Because I was bored and tired, the lecture went over my head.
4.
5. Because I played frisbie all evening, I did not get my English paper finished.
6.
7. I saw the broken ladder leaning against the barn.
8. After watching TV all evening, I found the dirty dishes still on the table.
9. When I was six, my grandfather paid us a visit.
10. Looking out the window, I could see the plane.

EXERCISE 3

1. I brought the dog, badly in need of a bath, into the laundry room.
2. A boy hit me in the face with a pomegranate skin.
3. Dressed in a long blue evening gown, she seemed to him prettier than ever.
4.
5. We watched the first spring warblers darting here and there through the bushes.
6. I stopped and talked to the child, who was crying pitifully.
7. Sitting beside the hotel window, we could see the entire ski tournament.
8.
9. As he stepped on the gas, the car shot forward.

10. Hoping it would quit raining by the next day, we postponed the picnic.

EXERCISE 4

1. While driving along in the car, we saw a deer run across the road.
2. We could see little white pieces of paper falling from the Empire State Building.
3. While she was on a two-week vacation, the office had to take care of itself.
4. I saw in the evening paper that the murderer had been captured.
5. Driving as fast as possible, we finally reached the hospital.
6. The car I bought from a used-car dealer had a leaky radiator.
7. Sitting out there in the stadium, the fans must have had to have a lot of blankets.
8. Apologetically she placed the food before us.
9. While we talked to one another, our ideas became clear.
10. With threats and promises, Dad urged me to finish my college career.

EXERCISE 5

1. While tobogganing down the hill, we saw a huge bear come out of the woods.
2. He suddenly noticed a stop sign gleaming red in the sunlight.
3.
4. The monkey watched us as it peeled a banana in the cage.
5. I tried to quiet the screaming and kicking child.
6.
7. Rocking back and forth, she did not disclose her thoughts.
8.
9. Having worked hard all day, I let the lawn go without mowing.
10. Suddenly becoming frightened, she imagined the house was full of noises.

EXERCISE 6

1. Because I went to too many parties, my term paper was late.
2. Because the child had narrowly missed being run over, I gave him some advice about crossing streets.
3. Groping around in the dark for the switch, he overturned the coffee table.
4. Having finished eating, we left the table bare.
5.
6. Because I was very tired, Mother told me I didn't need to help with the dishes.
7. As I lay there on the beach in the sun, school didn't seem important.
8.
9. We saw the parade moving slowly down the street.
10.

EXERCISE 7

1. As I put on the brakes quickly, the car screeched to a stop.
2. Consulting the Lost and Found section of the paper, we soon had the dog safe at home again.
3.
4. On her new dress was a spot that could not be removed.
5. Skidding to a stop, our car barely missed hitting an old lady.
6.
7. I lost a pen that did not belong to me out of my briefcase.
8. I decided to give the clothes I had no use for to a charity.
9. Although his car was almost eight years old, he refused to turn it in on a later model.
10. In the lapel of his coat we noticed a small flower that she no doubt had given him.

EXERCISE 8

1. I saw the cat purring contentedly in my armchair.
2. A son weighing eight pounds was born to Mr. and Mrs. N. L. Smith.
3. I don't enjoy his company because he's a bore.
4. I don't care for cucumbers unless they are pickled.
5. Discouraged, I let the book and all the notes fall to the floor.
6. Almost too excited to eat, I read the letter over and over.
7. As she jumped the little creek, she noticed a large bed of violets.
8. Shivering with cold, he ran up the steps and into the deserted house.
9. The series of lectures we are having on religions of the world will end on May 30.
10. She put the sandwiches that she had not eaten back into the bag.

EXERCISE 9

1. After she had driven a thousand miles, her children welcomed her home.
2. When I was three, my father took me to the city for the first time.
3. Having been born and raised in the country, I naturally find the old cookstove appealing.
4. Excited and eager to go, we saw the bus waiting for us in front of the building.
5. The house where I was born is surrounded by a grove of catalpa trees.
6. After a three-year absence, we found that the trees were full grown.
7. As they unwrapped gift after gift, the puppy had a great time playing with all the tissue paper.
8. Zooming down the hill, we struck the tree with a bang.
9. After eating lunch hurriedly, we started in two taxis for Yosemite.
10. The park seat made a good resting-place for the discouraged tramp.

EXERCISE 10

1. The youngster went careening down the driveway on a scooter just as we arrived.

2. I watched the horses in the pasture quietly munching hay.
3. Wagging its tail, the little black dog followed him.
4. Marching down the aisle, the bride tripped on the rug.
5. While I talked on the phone, the cake burned.
6. I realized my parents had raised me with love and care in the best way they could.
7. Lincoln Park is the most interesting park I have seen in the city.
8. She was engaged to a man named Smith, who had a Cougar.
9. When I was fourteen, my sister was born.
10. We gave all the food we didn't want to the dog.

Getting Rid of Faulty References (p. 93)

EXERCISE 1

1. I put the omelet on the table, took off my apron, and began to eat.
2. The government has established schools where cooking, interior decorating, and household management are taught.
3. My family was annoyed because I decided not to get a summer job.
4. She asked her sister, "Why wasn't I invited to the party?"
5. Jay was allowed to take his father's new tennis racket to school.
6. She offered to let her roommate wear her red dress.
7. The president said to the dean, "You have been too lenient."
8. To be a good fraternity brother, you must cooperate with any project the members undertake.
9. The teachers established a play center where the children can spend their leisure.
10. Ray said to the professor, "Your watch is wrong."

EXERCISE 2

1. When I picked up the dog's dish, the dog began to bark.
2. Because I have always been interested in coaching football ever since I was in high school, I have decided to become a coach.
3.
4. I enjoyed my month in Japan. The Japanese are very artistic people.
5. The chairwoman said, "Please keep your secret from the others."
6. Sandra said to Janice, "You are wasting your time studying music."
7. I have a pair of glasses, but my eyes are so good that I don't use the glasses except for reading.
8. Although I had never been fishing before, I caught a fish immediately.
9. She likes to swim; in fact she spends most of her summer swimming.
10. She was chosen student body president because she is good in her studies even though she is not very good in sports.

EXERCISE 3

1. He said to his boss, "Will I have to make out a claim sheet concerning the accident?"
2. Since we couldn't find the cake plate, we realized the children must have eaten the cake.
3. Her mother said to her, "I'll have to be more considerate."
4. The naturalist showed us his collection of birds' nests and told us how the birds build them.
5. I have adjusted the steering wheel, and you can take your car home anytime.
6. After I had read the story of Lindbergh's life, I decided I wanted to be an airline pilot.

7. He said to the man, "Won't you come back when I have time to talk?"
8. Jerome was very angry when he talked to his father.
9. Refusing to promote the new invention hurt their business.
10. His father said, "I'll have to try to get a more modern view."

EXERCISE 4

1. Andy said to his brother, "Your car has a flat tire."
2. I enjoy prizefights and would like to be a prizefighter if I could.
3. She said to her daughter, "You've always been a good cook."
4. In China the main food is rice.
5. I should have followed my father's wise advice.
6. Mrs. Smith said to Mrs. Brown, "Your dog is in my yard."
7. The cars whizzed past, but no one even looked my way.
8. As soon as I approached the robin's nest, the robin flew away.
9. It wasn't easy for Sarah to explain to the instructor that she had lost the term paper she had written.
10. She said to her roommate, "You are spending too much time going to parties."

EXERCISE 5

1. He said, "Dad, you need a new suit."
2. He said to his professor, "Why can't you understand my essay?"
3. He said to his roommate, "I'm a time waster."
4. Hawaii is a beautiful state where no billboards are allowed.
5. My math teacher gave me a low grade because I was really poor in math.
6. He said to his father, "I ought to wash the car."
7. I walked into the room, climbed on the ladder, and began to paint the ceiling.
8. The professor said to him, "Your article is going to be published."
9. Ben said, "Dad, you ought to get a refund for the faulty tire."
10. When I opened the door of the birdcage, the bird flew out.

EXERCISE 6

1. Trying to decide what trip to take isn't easy.
2. It would be cold in New England at this time of year, and I don't like the cold.
3. He asked the mechanic, "Why am I having trouble?"
4. As soon as Dad had put in the new battery, I went whizzing off in the car.
5. He complained, "Dad, your car is an antique."
6. I have always liked French Provincial furniture and have finally decided to buy a French Provincial dresser.
7. She said to her instructor, "You don't understand what I'm saying."
8. Al complained that Mark was extravagant.

9. She said to her mother, "I think I need a physical checkup."
10. I really liked the two textbooks we had to read.

EXERCISE 7

1. The child screamed when I moved his tricycle.
2. In *Brave New World* Huxley describes many things that have come true today.
3. Lauren said, "Mother, my dresses are all dated."
4.
5. The car hit the bridge railing but was not damaged.
6. I was impressed with how friendly the girls were at the sorority rush party.
7. We spent our vacation in Nassau, where the climate is delightful.
8. I thought he would phone, and I waited all evening for the phone to ring.
9. I've decided to save all my money for a trip although it won't be easy.
10. He admitted to his twin brother that he had been at fault.

EXERCISE 8

1. Because he missed the curve, his motorcycle swerved into the side of a house, but the house was not damaged.
2. As I approached the playpen, the baby began to cry.
3. As soon as the fender was repaired, I drove the car home.
4. The instructor said, "I don't understand the poem."
5. His father said to him, "I think you should carry more insurance."
6.
7. I liked California except for the smog.
8. She said to her visitor, "Come back when I have had more time to study the project."
9. The boss was really despondent when he talked with Mac.
10. She said to her roommate, "My stereo needs a new needle."

EXERCISE 9

1. The child was pleased when I praised his finger painting.
2. I was pleased that they offered me a job.
3. The instructor said, "My explanation was faulty."
4. As I tried to attach the leash, the dog jumped away.
5. I really liked having only six students in that class.
6. It was good that I had refused to follow his suggestion.
7. Her counselor said, "You need more time to think about the question."
8.
9. She said to her mother, "You need to be positive before making such a big decision."

10. We couldn't find a single bottle and blamed Mike for drinking all the cokes.

EXERCISE 10

1. The chairman said, "Please reconsider your statement."
2. Her roommate came in crying at four a.m.
3. His dad said, "I'll have to be more generous with my time."
4. She showed us her shell collection and explained how the small animals live in the shells.
5. The parents take turns at the playground, where their children can use the slides, swings, and teeter-totters.
6. David said to his instructor, "I am confused about the novel."
7. Their refusing to give me any more money was just the push I needed.
8. The salesman said to his supervisor, "I have been negligent in my job."
9. I was asked to serve on the committee but felt the committee was unnecessary.
10. She asked her mother to have a little better sense of humor in the future.

Making Subjects, Verbs, and Pronouns Agree (p. 102)

EXERCISE 1

1. is, his
2. was
3. doesn't
4. walked, asked
5. are
6. were
7. are
8. were
9. goes, doesn't
10. Doesn't

EXERCISE 2

1. was, its
2. has, her
3. have
4. requires, doesn't
5. were, were
6. is
7. doesn't
8. have
9. presents
10. were

EXERCISE 3

1. is
2. were
3. his, is
4. doesn't
5. has
6. was
7. contain
8. exhibits
9. are
10. was

EXERCISE 4

1. doesn't
2. were
3. were
4. are
5. were
6. is, his
7. was
8. were, walked
9. is
10. is

EXERCISE 5

1. are
2. were, was
3. Doesn't
4. were
5. doesn't
6. is
7. walk, walked
8. were
9. was
10. were

EXERCISE 6

1. are, expect
2. passed, refuse
3. were
4. cooks
5. was
6. doesn't
7. remain
8. doesn't
9. used, haven't
10. have

EXERCISE 7

1. doesn't
2. wanted, were
3. are
4. are
5. have

6. is
7. Doesn't
8. talked, asked, cooked
9. were
10. doesn't

EXERCISE 8

1. Weren't
2. are
3. were
4. were
5. were

6. wonder, dropped
7. doesn't
8. is
9. were
10. Doesn't

EXERCISE 9

1. moved, seems
2. fulfills, contains
3. doesn't
4. were, weren't
5. walked, were

6. walk, are
7. has, his
8. Doesn't
9. scared
10. has, its

EXERCISE 10

1. discussed, interests
2. analyzed, used
3. impressed
4. Doesn't
5. walks

6. fascinate, want
7. follow, hope
8. has
9. Were, played
10. canvassed

Choosing the Right Pronoun (p. 107)

EXERCISE 1

1. me
2. him
3. me
4. him
5. He, I

6. me
7. me
8. us
9. me
10. her

EXERCISE 2

1. me
2. us
3. him
4. him
5. he

6. me
7. us
8. her
9. he
10. We

EXERCISE 3

1. me
2. me
3. We
4. me
5. me

6. me
7. him
8. him
9. me
10. her

EXERCISE 4

1. me
2. her
3. she
4. us
5. he

6. us
7. me
8. we
9. she
10. We

EXERCISE 5

1. us
2. me
3. him
4. he
5. We

6. us
7. me
8. I
9. us
10. I

EXERCISE 6

1. he
2. me
3. me
4. her
5. him

6. he
7. me
8. I
9. me
10. me

EXERCISE 7

1. him
2. he
3. They, I
4. her
5. us

6. he
7. I
8. We
9. they
10. we

EXERCISE 8

1. Alec and I
2. I
3. us
4. me
5. I

6. he
7. me
8. I
9. me
10. he

EXERCISE 9

1. me
2. I
3. us
4. I
5. I

6. We
7. me
8. me
9. them, us
10. us

EXERCISE 10

1. us
2. us
3. he
4. me
5. she

6. My kid brother and I
7. I
8. she
9. me
10. us

Using Parallel Construction (p. 112)

EXERCISE 1

1. and sleeping
2. and exhaustion during
3. or making an oral report
4. that is not too long
5. or a doctor
6. and with modern conveniences
7. then making an exhibit
8. and studied
9. and packed the car
10. and too many misspelled words

EXERCISE 2

1. and to eat plenty of fresh
2. and has a good sense
3. and yet to increase
4. and faultfinding
5. coping with a new job
6. and mild weather
7. and long-winded
8. the pleasant boss
9. joining a sorority
10. and to give my name and age

EXERCISE 3

1. and camping out
2. and to get along
3. nor how much it costs
4. and bubble gum
5. and to perform
6. how to decorate a house and how to choose colors, fabrics, furniture, and rugs
7. and took pictures
8. and playing tennis
9. scratching
10. and to value

EXERCISE 4

1. horses to curry
2. and etching
3. than to have
4. and riding horseback
5. and entertaining
6. and their ability to resist
7. and oversensitiveness
8. and to read better books
9. and concluded with
10. often rainy

EXERCISE 5

1. and for the new hospital bond issue too
2. and a vest
3. and understanding
4.
5. and security
6. and he has never supported education bills
7. and a good activity record
8. and too much noise
9. even going for a hike
10. and miner

EXERCISE 6

1. and to come when called
2. and went to bed
3. inches wide
4. to have a vacation and to paint
5. and who has had a great deal
6.
7. but not to vote
8. and in one corner her bulging file cabinet
9. and was made
10. and even did

EXERCISE 7

1. and waited
2. and the increase in crime
3. and by air
4. or a musician
5. but likable

6. and by cooking economy meals
7. and interesting illustrations
8. is required but also
9.
10. and how to change a tire

EXERCISE 8

1. and unnecessary
2. and rewriting
3. and tact
4. and cleaning
5. and organize

6. and that I should not worry
7. and open-fire cooking
8. about our interests, our families, and our courses
9. and to have physical strength
10. how to prepare the meal, or how to use her stove

EXERCISE 9

1. and a marble inlay from India
2. and his dependability
3.
4.
5. and by taking him on

6. and his warm friendliness
7.
8. and some snacks nearby
9. and all kinds of flowers
10. and sometimes even sat and enjoyed them

EXERCISE 10

1. Every college student should know how to type because
   1. some instructors require typed papers
   2. typing, if one is good at it, saves time
   3. a typed paper often gets a higher grade

2. Going home every weekend is unwise because
   1. I spend too much time on the bus
   2. I get behind in my college work
   3. it is too expensive
   4. I miss out on weekend activities at college

3. Commercial billboards along highways should be prohibited because
   1. they often cause accidents
   2. they mar the scenery

4. Learning to sew is valuable because
   1. sewing your own clothes saves money
   2. sewing teaches you to be creative

5. My chief objectives in this course are
   1. to learn to spell
   2. to learn to write well-constructed sentences
   3. to learn to write a clear composition

Avoiding Shift in Tense (p. 121)

EXERCISE 1

1. saw, looked
2. said
3. walks
4. said
5. stop, see
6. drops
7. tells
8. said
9. said
10. is

EXERCISE 2

1. turns
2. stop, wait
3. walked
4. comes
5. was
6. happened
7. were, wasn't
8. gave
9. watched
10. told

EXERCISE 3

1. didn't, didn't
2. says, help
3. escapes
4. discovered, hadn't
5. came
6. showed, was
7. turns, walks
8. came, turned
9. have
10. went

EXERCISE 4

1. becomes
2. thinks, becomes
3. fell
4. heard, came
5. is
6. came
7. can't
8. writes
9. walks
10. sat

EXERCISE 5

1. said
2. spied
3. couldn't
4. was, got
5. said I was
6. had
7. realized
8. get
9. got
10. spotted, could

EXERCISE 6

1. went
2. surprised
3. wrote bits of
4. had
5. comes
6. decides
7. got
8. came
9. didn't
10. tells

EXERCISE 7

1. punished
2. says, can't
3. can
4. run
5. gets
6. saw
7. have
8. crawled
9. remembered
10. asked, could

EXERCISE 8

1. looked
2. came
3. is
4. came
5. gave, had
6. give, sit, listen
7. came
8. loved
9. came
10. brings, is

EXERCISE 9

. . . My mother stood . . . she was afraid I was. . . . I finally got it up.
. . . I was listening to radios . . . Eventually I decided I wanted. . . .
Mostly I just listened and worked. . . .

EXERCISE 10

. . . I signaled. . . . I started the turn. . . . I pulled off the road. . . . I
stopped the truck and got out. . . .

Avoiding Shift in Person (p. 130)

EXERCISE 1

1. their equipment
2. he isn't going
3. he enters
4. he really tries and is willing to take what he
5. he is sure
6. you should
7. he wants
8. I have to be
9. to help me
10. he will

EXERCISE 2

1. he doesn't have
2. he won't
3.
4. I really had to have guts to leave my
5. we could
6. we could
7. we got
8. he wants
9. he has to stick
10. he has to be

EXERCISE 3

1. they have to set
2. He should learn to allot his *or* One should learn to allot his
3. He can improve his vocabulary if he works
4. he is
5. he has
6. he has
7. one can't
8. he is sure to get behind in his
9. one naturally
10. he should

EXERCISE 4

1. he may not see
2. he is
3. one has
4. he should
5. he would
6. he should
7. you should
8. your car
9. he will
10. One should use a good grade of paint and should not

EXERCISE 5

1. you expect
2. his ticket
3. he simply watches his
4. he reads
5. his luggage
6. he wants his
7. I have
8. with me
9. he won't
10. we could

EXERCISE 6

1. we couldn't
2. he will
3. one has not
4. he has to . . . make up his mind that he really intends
5. he can't
6. he wants
7. he just gives
8. one can't . . . his first term
9. he simply decides . . . he learns
10. he spends

EXERCISE 7

1. we could
2. we grew up, we became
3. one learns
4. I really
5. if he does, he simply reinforces
6. you should
7. me a chance
8. you want
9. my brain
10. he wants

EXERCISE 8

1. I'd get paid
2. your life
3. What he learns . . . on his mind
4. You should get more involved
5. in which I made a piece of furniture. I did this on my own

EXERCISE 9

1. If one has to . . . he gets closer . . . He becomes
2. He has to get used
3. I feel fulfilled.
4. I never get
5. I gained confidence from the experience.

EXERCISE 10

she should ask . . . to put her to sleep painlessly. No person has the right to take another man's life. The only person . . . unless he's the Creator. . . .

Getting Rid of Wordiness (p. 138)

EXERCISE 1

1. She looks best in her brown suit.
2. I consider him a genius.
3. The class president appointed him class representative.
4. I woke up at four this morning.
5. I was as good in sports as my brother.
6. I am taking math and physics.
7. The custom is to give everyone a gift the day a new store opens.
8. My small brother had big ideas.
9. You don't have to refer to history to see examples of bribery.
10. His prospects are probably few.

EXERCISE 2

1. Another athlete threw the discus ten yards.
2. At six a.m. we saw a perfect sunrise.
3. Today we are surrounded with crime.
4. In 1975 nothing was done to solve the problem.
5. Since an innovation is being used in production, the product should be better.
6. We decided then to move our office.
7. Since I had missed several classes, I knew I would fail.
8. We were considering whether to charge admission.
9. My father loves football.
10. My girl friend is unique.

EXERCISE 3

1. Many will agree with this point; many will disagree.
2. The story made me feel a part of it.
3. It seemed as if it had happened to me.
4. He had committed all kinds of crimes and yet was allowed to go free.
5. The department had chosen this girl as their representative.
6. The club members decided to clean up the park.
7. I considered it a worthwhile project.
8. Many people never read a book.
9. His height makes him a good basketball player.
10. The melons were large and sweet.

EXERCISE 4

1. His attitude was puzzling.
2. I am taking money out of my account to buy my books.
3. I don't like that course because I don't understand it.
4. After our eight-hour hike, we were hungry.
5. He had tried football, basketball, and hockey.

6. We discussed having certain floors designated as quiet floors, where no radios or TVs could be played during study hours.
7. My mother always gives me a lot of instructions when I am going out the door.
8. No one should decide what career another should enter.
9. I was astounded at the way she took charge of the house, the meals, and the children.
10. You must first work out a thesis statement and then find specific details to support it.

EXERCISE 5

1. Finally you should learn more at college than just what you learn from your courses.
2. It was a square cake with candles.
3. Most people consider the architecture on our campus impressive.
4. Since I did not hand my paper in on time, I probably won't pass the course.
5. I am tired of the course.
6. Although I reviewed thoroughly, I failed the exam.
7. I had wanted an *A* in that course.
8. Now I am not going to get an *A*.
9. Will you be a candidate for vice-president of our club?
10. If he does not come to dinner, we will be short one hand at bridge.

EXERCISE 6

1. He can be depended upon to do what he says he will.
2. He thought the Democrats would win.
3. Most students do not leave campus on weekends.
4. He did not consider her record.
5. He really wanted to fire her.
6. The board had to decide whether to support the dean's action.
7. Because I was younger than the other contestants, I felt inferior.
8. A number are planning to take the alumni tour to England.
9. It was three a.m. when we finally arrived.
10. The three kinds of shells we found were unique.

EXERCISE 7

1. A lot of people were there.
2. In April ten people were hurt in accidents in the city.
3. At present thousands of acres are under water along the river.
4. I think something should be done to prevent flooding.
5. No one seems to be working on the problem.
6. We should refer to our parents' days to see how much better off we are than they were.
7. Many people do not appreciate the good things about our day.

8. For example modern medicine has increased man's life-span by a number of years.
9. Finally the doctor arrived but could do nothing for her.
10. The plane circled the airport for half an hour and then disappeared.

EXERCISE 8

1. One solution is as good as the other.
2. I've decided I'm not interested in the job.
3. Ten players were suspended.
4. They shuttled between their country home and their city apartment.
5. A friend of mine has made an invention.
6. I have tried to collect all the information I will need, and I hope the result will be satisfactory.
7. They carried him home drunk.
8. No doubt our team will win.
9. He has worked hard all his life.
10. Math bores me.

EXERCISE 9

1. I was unaware that she had arrived.
2. Because he had not planned his talk, it was monotonous.
3. I grew up in an ordinary home.
4. Justice is too slow in this country.
5. Justice should be swift and sure.
6. The tale I am going to tell you is unbelievable.
7. In September everyone comes back to the campus.
8. He left college because he wanted some business experience.
9. I have had no time to finish my paper.
10. When I finish it, it will be the best paper I can write.

EXERCISE 10

To help new students find their way around the Library, the staff offers orientation programs. Many faculty members also bring their classes to particular subject areas for orientation, and printed handouts, such as special subject bibliographies and instructions on the use of periodical indexes or psychological abstracts, are available.

Punctuation (p. 149)

EXERCISE 1

1. Hurry! We've only two minutes until takeoff time.
2. We identified three new birds that day: a golden-crowned kinglet, a field sparrow, and a hermit thrush.
3. He asked whether we had seen her.
4. Did he bring what you wanted from the city?
5. We took her everything we thought a sick person might like: books, flowers, fruit, and the latest magazines.
6. The meeting was called for three p.m.; it began at four.
7. Didn't you know she had gone?
8. Why didn't you answer my letters?
9. Go away! I want to work.
10. You can reach him if you call before eight a.m.

EXERCISE 2

1. Our candidate will be at the party; therefore I want to go.
2. The recipe calls for the following ingredients: butter, milk, eggs, salt, and slices of bread.
3. Why were you absent from class?
4. The package was sent C.O.D.
5. I asked him why he didn't come last night.
6. Why don't you apply for the job?
7. Hey! I almost forgot I've invited guests to dinner.
8. What a stupid thing to do!
9. Will you sing for me?
10. Why he hasn't come is a mystery to me.

EXERCISE 3

1. Why don't they stop this racket?
2. He received his B.A. last June; now he is working for his M.A.
3. A letter consists of the following parts: heading, salutation, body, and conclusion.
4. We walked through the deep woods to the creek; then we sat down to watch the waterfowl.
5. I'm taking English, American history, political science, and French.
6. I'm taking the following subjects: English, American history, political science, and French.
7. What a commotion!
8. What about Tommy? Where's he?
9. He asked why we had done nothing to stop the story.
10. Why didn't you go with your brother?

EXERCISE 4

1. Not a trace of the old farm was left; the buildings had all been leveled and corn planted where they once stood.

2. They had no plans for the summer; therefore we went to visit them.
3. Why has it taken so long for him to get back?
4. The cast includes the following students: Craig, Stanley, Rita, and Kevin.
5. The cast includes Craig, Stanley, Rita, and Kevin.
6. The candidate's strong points are the following: sincerity, adaptability, and dependability.
7. Everyone was concerned; everyone offered to help.
8. At the auction she bought a sofa, two old chairs, and a popcorn popper.
9. He asked whether he might join the party.
10. The magazine contained stories, essays, and verse.

EXERCISE 5

1. Have you ever taken karate lessons?
2. Their petition asked for three things: shorter hours, double pay for overtime, and two-week summer vacations.
3. I asked the policeman whether we could park inside the grounds.
4. What do they expect us to do?
5. He visited the following parks: Yellowstone, Glacier, and Sequoia.
6. He visited Yellowstone, Glacier, and Sequoia parks.
7. How can you walk in all that wind?
8. Look! It's a sparrow hawk hanging in midair.
9. Do you mean I'm supposed to sit here all day?
10. I was awakened at four a.m. by shouts below my window: I got up hurriedly and dressed.

EXERCISE 6

1. Stop! You are ruining the picture.
2. When the moon is fullest, it begins to wane; when it is darkest, it begins to grow.
3. She had all that money could buy: home, servants, clothes, and cars.
4. Help! I've lost Archie.
5. I studied until three a.m.; then I went to bed.
6. Isn't it about time he finished college?
7. He wanted to know whether I had a scholarship.
8. It takes two things to learn to spell: determination and drill.
9. He took the following courses in his freshman year: English, ecomomics, chemistry, and gym.
10. The most famous English novelists of the nineteenth century are Dickens, Scott, and Thackeray.

EXERCISE 7

1. We worked at party headquarters all morning; then we canvassed all afternoon.
2. The driver suddenly shifted gears; then he stepped on the gas and was off in a cloud of dust.

3. Does anyone have his car available?
4. A person usually minimizes his own mistakes; he magnifies those of others.
5. They plan to visit the following countries: New Zealand, Australia, and Japan.
6. I worked for a year after finishing high school; therefore I won't graduate from college when my friends do.
7. Who has left his books in my locker?
8. I like the country roads with their sumac and bittersweet; they remind me of my childhood.
9. The snow was deep and crusty; it was a perfect day for skiing.
10. Wait! I'm coming too.

EXERCISE 8

1. He was correct; that was exactly what I wanted to do.
2. Couldn't he play, or didn't he want to play?
3. The last race was about to start; my confidence was building.
4. Then came trouble; in order to avoid a collision I had to go over the starting line.
5. Slam! Unexpectedly a steel gate closed in front of me.
6. He asked whether I had seen Ron.
7. I finally found Ron; he was in great spirits.
8. This lesson includes the following punctuation marks: period, question mark, exclamation mark, semicolon, and colon.
9. Wonderful! That's just what I need!
10. The dainty Maryland yellowthroat warbled beside the stream.

EXERCISE 9

1. She asked me what I thought of Degas.
2. During our days on the beach we picked up many kinds of shells: conchs, cowries, limpets, oysters, and whelks.
3. He had received his A.B., his M.A., and his Ph.D. before he was thirty.
4. Did you phone me last night?
5. Thornton Wilder wrote the following successful plays: *Our Town, The Skin of our Teeth,* and *The Long Christmas Dinner.*
6. They are going to the play, aren't they?
7. Dan asked me if I intended to stay on the committee.
8. A number of birds have visited my feeder all winter: juncos, nuthatches, chickadees, and jays.
9. I am interested in a number of career possibilities: law, business, and teaching.
10. Help! Can anyone tell me how to start this paper?

EXERCISE 10

1. From nine a.m. to six p.m. I slept.
2. Don't tell me what to do!

3. "Quit it!" he shouted.
4. She sat there trying to decide whether to order chicken, lobster, or a steak.
5. The fall quarter begins on September 5 and ends on November 28.
6. The most unusual buildings in town are the courthouse, the old one-room schoolhouse, and the Thatcher residence.
7. Hey! Give me a hand!
8. Her many duties included supervising personnel, reporting on projects, and attending board meetings.
9. They asked whether they were intruding.
10. The course was too difficult; I soon gave up.

Commas (p. 154)

EXERCISE 1

1. It was an exhausting,
2. You'd better learn to rewrite,
3. I write and write and rewrite,
4. Pipelines, highways,
5. They traced him as far as Tucson, Arizona,
6.
7.
8.
9. England, France,
10. The greatest loss of life in the history of the world occurred in the earthquake in Shensi Province, China, on January 23, 1556,

EXERCISE 2

1. Her address was 4530 Evans Avenue, Chicago,
2. She was intelligent, charming,
3. He is an eye, ear, nose,
4. You may write to him in care of American Express, Buenos Aires,
5. Spinach is supposed to be healthful,
6. We made the lunch, packed the car,
7. He thinks he can predict the weather,
8. The armistice after World War I was proclaimed on November 11, 1918.
9. You can get the document by writing to the Superintendent of Documents, Government Printing Office, Washington,
10. I've learned to avoid fragments, run-together sentences,

EXERCISE 3

1. John Lees of Brighton, England, walked 2,976 miles from Los Angeles to New York City in 53 days, 12 hours,
2. He was looking for an investment that offered a chance of growth, high interest,
3.
4. Alaska was purchased from Russia on March 30,
5.
6. On April 8, 1513, Ponce de Leon landed at St. Augustine,
7. I looked in every store in town,
8. From September 2 to September 6, 1665,
9. Jim hoped someone would come to relieve him,
10. He was too much interested in cars, movies,

EXERCISE 4

1. On the plate were celery, olives,
2. The three levels of government in the United States are local, state,

3. She wore a black suit, brown shoes,
4. The Stars and Stripes flag was adopted by the Continental Congress on June 14,
5.
6. I finished all my work, cleared my desk,
7.
8. I had always been an eager,
9. The Panama Canal was opened on August 15,
10.

EXERCISE 5

1. I have done my homework for tomorrow,
2. We were careful to mark our trail,
3. Lincoln made his Gettysburg Address on November 19,
4. The dull,
5. He slung his ice pick, his oxygen mask,
6. We wanted to attend the lecture series,
7. It was difficult to support her husband, her son,
8. The chairman appointed committees on decoration, program,
9. Our class reunion was set for ten o'clock on Saturday morning,
10.

EXERCISE 6

1.
2. Walt Whitman was born near Huntington, Long Island, May 31, 1819, and died on March 26,
3. Could you meet me at Field's at noon on Tuesday,
4. The office is located on the ninth floor of the Hart Building,
5.
6. He had studied a great deal about the English, American,
7.
8.
9. The three conifers in my yard are a blue spruce, a cedar,
10. Although known as the chief interpreter of New England, Robert Frost was born in San Francisco, California, March 26,

EXERCISE 7

1. We couldn't do the decorating without a stepladder,
2.
3. No one really expected her to come,
4. The political machine controlled the newspapers, the courts,
5. The letter, yellow with age, was dated January 3,
6. The library displayed a number of manuscripts, letters,
7.
8. Taxicabs, limousines,

9. The exhibit included water colors, oils,
10. He couldn't decide whether to go into politics, business,

EXERCISE 8

1. Vachel Lindsay was born in Springfield, Illinois, on November 10, 1879,
2. She arranged the furniture, hung the pictures,
3. I used to drive a bright red Chevy,
4. A bore talks mostly in first person, a gossip in third,
5. Her mother was kind, soft-spoken,
6.
7. The child was surprised, hurt,
8. He had done the best he could in the course,
9. The fastest time for an around-the-world journey on commercial flights is 36 hours, 19 minutes,
10. You should spend more time on revising your essays,

EXERCISE 9

1. We visited Mexico, Guatemala,
2. She was the first president of the Columbus, Ohio,
3. We stayed at Camp Alinet, Devil's Lake, Minnesota,
4. He was the handsome, intelligent,
5. He won the local meet,
6.
7. The prime minister's address is 10 Downing Street, London,
8. About the only date in history that he was sure of was July 4,
9. We're leaving now,
10. They lived at 631 East Ayer, Ironwood, Michigan,

EXERCISE 10

1. We hoped to stop in Ogden, Utah,
2. She had never mopped a floor in her life,
3. Scandinavia is the ancient name of Sweden, Norway, Denmark,
4. New York, Chicago, Philadelphia, Detroit,
5. An awkward,
6. Every morning he had a breakfast of toast, coffee,
7. The road was narrow, muddy,
8. She got out of the car, slammed the door,
9. The new owners of the farm had no interest in the past,
10. The orchard, the hedge,

Commas (continued) (p. 159)

EXERCISE 1

1. Because there were no important issues,
2. We tried, however,
3. But however we tried,
4. Voters, it seems,
5. Taxation, to be sure,
6. The entire country, of course,
7. What we need, many think,
8. Swifter and surer punishment, they say,
9. Mr. Chairman,
10. Yes,

EXERCISE 2

1. Members of the Jury,
2.
3. Most of the jury members were, I think,
4. That company, it seems,
5. When I applied,
6. After I finish college,
7. Because many Americans are working shorter hours,
8. Many are turning to home gardening,
9. The zest for growing things, it seems,
10. Instead of watching TV,

EXERCISE 3

1. The program was, on the whole,
2. Betty,
3. No,
4. Yes, Warren,
5. However much you do,
6. It should not be imagined, however,
7. As I've told you before, Nancy,
8. Yes,
9. I'm sorry, Madam,
10. There are, on the other hand,

EXERCISE 4

1.
2. Because he was so determined to succeed,
3. Come on, gang,
4. We have, of course,
5. That was, I think,
6. I think, for example,

7. Isn't it odd, Ellen,
8. After you have finished ten sentences,
9. I'm hoping, Jean,
10. The car, it seems,

EXERCISE 5

1. We tried, nevertheless,
2. Your paper, on the whole,
3. Yes, it's much better, I think,
4. When I read my paper aloud,
5. Since I have learned to write a thesis statement,
6. Whenever I'm not sure of the spelling of a word,
7. Focused free writing, I find,
8. Even though I don't always like writing,
9. While I'm in college,
10. I've been trying out a few new recipes, however,

EXERCISE 6

1. He said, moreover,
2. Our craftsman will, I assure you,
3. There's more room in this car,
4. Come here, Debra,
5. Although we had a long way to go home,
6. Yes,
7. When I really work,
8. And we said, furthermore,
9. He had, despite his inexperience,
10. Yes,

EXERCISE 7

1. Our football coach is, I am sure,
2. You must not, on the other hand,
3. Conductor,
4. Sis,
5. When a dependent clause comes first in a sentence,
6. It seems likely, therefore,
7. A man's character and his garden, it has been said,
8. I tell you, Dale,
9. There are a few things, nevertheless,
10. Are you, then,

EXERCISE 8

1. The speech, on the contrary,
2. My interpretation of his speech is, I believe,
3. The farmers, it seems to me,

4. I thought we might, for example,
5. Well,
6. All right,
7. Well, fellows,
8. Remember, Beth,
9. Whenever I see crocuses,
10. The suit was, to be sure,

EXERCISE 9

1.
2. She was, beyond a doubt,
3. You should, I think,
4. The party, it seems to me,
5. You see, Marie,
6. Since I don't play bridge,
7. Wouldn't it be better, Dad,
8. When I entered,
9. I was positive, however,
10. The high grades, you will find,

EXERCISE 10

1. To improve your figure, Sue,
2. In the past, I am told,
3. The evidence, I suppose,
4. She did as well as she could, I think,
5. Who, by the way,
6. When you are sure you have a good thesis statement,
7.
8. As I entered,
9. She was, I think,
10. When I finished,

Commas (continued) (p. 163)

EXERCISE 1

1.
2. My mother, who bakes the best pies in town,
3.
4.
5. Several of the books of Charles Dickens, a nineteenth-century author,
6.
7.
8. The cat, having lapped up its milk,
9. The night shift, which did not end until midnight,
10. Sandy, who thinks she looks like a movie star,

EXERCISE 2

1. He went to his summer home,
2. My brother, trying out his new bicycle,
3.
4. His home life, which was remarkably placid,
5. The president's letter, which had been missent,
6.
7. The two longest rivers in the world are the Amazon, flowing into the South Atlantic, and the Nile,
8. Lucien Smith, my piano instructor,
9.
10. My roommate, who lives in Chicago,

EXERCISE 3

1. Have you ever read *I'm OK—You're OK*,
2. On the next morning, January 23,
3.
4. Mr. Cox, who is my favorite prof,
5.
6. My client, Mr. Hawk,
7. Her mother, a very intelligent woman,
8.
9. The rest of the passengers, who were forced to listen,
10.

EXERCISE 4

1. Mrs. Janice James, wife of a steel mill laborer,
2. Have you ever been in Minnesota,
3. Kilauea, which was active when we were in Hawaii,
4. We have decided to get Eddie Gray's orchestra,

5.

6.

7. The *Queen Mary*, which is now a Long Beach tourist attraction,

8. Bill, who had almost fallen asleep,

9. Marcia, who is the youngest in the group,

10.

EXERCISE 5

1.

2. This suit, which I bought before Easter,

3. More than a hundred years ago Hanson Gregory, captain of a schooner and dabbler in the culinary art,

4.

5. Don Johnson, captain of the basketball team,

6.

7. The Civil Aeronautics Board, appointed to regulate the aviation industry,

8.

9.

10. Maxie, who is my best friend,

EXERCISE 6

1. Everyone liked our prom decorations,

2.

3. My cousin Doris, who is spending the winter in Florida,

4.

5. Curtis Smith, whom I had met only the day before,

6. Just then in came Jamie,

7. Pamela Sterling, who is a member of the championship tennis team,

8.

9. The hunchback of Notre Dame, who was called Quasimodo the One-eyed,

10.

EXERCISE 7

1. The midterm examination, which will cover the information in the last five chapters,

2.

3. The photography contest, which is open to all students,

4. The anticlimax, which had seriously weakened the plot of the book,

5. The city of Nassau is located on the island of New Providence,

6. Williamsburg, which was at one time the capital of Virginia,

7.

8.

9.

10.

EXERCISE 8

1. Wayne, who had grown up in a poor home,
2.
3.
4. Living in the dormitory, even with its disadvantages,
5.
6.
7.
8.
9. Her grandmother's treadle sewing machine, which had been in use for more than fifty years,
10.

EXERCISE 9

1. *Walden,* which has become a classic,
2.
3.
4. The largest and heaviest animal in the world, and probably the biggest creature that ever existed,
5.
6. Arnold, who used to be an English teacher,
7.
8. Mike, who is an authority on birds,
9. George Bernard Shaw, who became one of England's most famous writers,
10. James Thurber, who was best known for his cartoons,

EXERCISE 10

1. *Ulysses,* a novel by James Joyce,
2. Ernest Hemingway, author of *A Farewell to Arms* and *For Whom the Bell Tolls,*
3. My cousin Pete, who owns a farm near the city,
4. The Amos Place, a quarter acre of unspoiled timber,
5. My older brother, who has been studying agriculture,
6. Her living room, which she had decorated herself,
7.
8.
9. The team, which had really worked hard all season,
10.

Quotation Marks (p. 170)

EXERCISE 1

1. "Isn't it too stormy to walk?" she asked.
2. "I'm too tired to go to the game," he said. "I think I'll watch it on TV."
3. "I hope you have enjoyed your work," said the superintendent.
4. "We haven't any red jackets," said the clerk. "Would you care to look at some other color?"
5. "One does not complain about water because it is wet, nor about rocks because they are hard," said Abraham Maslow.
6. "Nearly all men can stand adversity, but if you want to test a man's character, give him power," said Lincoln.
7.
8. "Can't you wait for us?" she pleaded. "We won't be long."
9. "No," she declared, "I won't vote for him. I won't vote for such a man!"
10. "The actions of some children," said Will Rogers, "suggest that their parents embarked on the sea of matrimony without a paddle."

EXERCISE 2

1. Alan Simpson gives this advice to young writers: "The first rule in English composition: every slaughtered syllable is a good deed."
2. La Rochefoucauld said, "As it is the mark of great minds to say many things in a few words, so it is the mark of little minds to use many words to say nothing."
3. "I won't be home until late," she said, "because I'm going to canvass for the Heart Fund."
4. "Doing work I like is more important to me than making a lot of money," she said.
5. "Hello," he said. "How are you?"
6. "Do you really want to know how I am?" she asked.
7. "A man is rich," said Henry David Thoreau, "in proportion to the number of things he can afford to let alone."
8. Viewing the multitude of articles exposed for sale in the market place, Socrates remarked, "How many things there are that I do not want."
9.
10. "The best time to tackle a small problem," said my father, "is before he grows up."

EXERCISE 3

1. Mark Twain said, "When I was a boy of fourteen, my father was so ignorant I could hardly stand to have the old man around. But when I got to be twenty-one, I was astonished at how much the old man had learned in seven years."

2. Mark Twain said, "The parts of the Bible which give me the most trouble are those I understand the best."
3. "Work consists of whatever a body is obliged to do, and play consists of whatever a body is not obliged to do," said Mark Twain.
4. I agree with the Spanish proverb, "How beautiful it is to do nothing and then rest afterward."
5. "When Mom goes shopping," said Kip, "she leaves no store unturned."
6. He found her munching chocolates and reading a book entitled *Eat, Drink, and Be Buried.*
7. "Finish every day and be done with it," said Ralph Waldo Emerson. "Tomorrow is a new day."
8. "Life can only be understood backward, but it must be lived forward," said Kierkegaard.
9. George Bernard Shaw said, "Few people think more than two or three times a year. I have made an international reputation for myself by thinking once or twice a week."
10. "The mind is everything," said Buddha. "What you think you become."

EXERCISE 4

1. "I'm sorry, but I can't stay," her visitor said, "because I must catch the 4:15 bus."
2. "Why don't you help with the day care center?" she asked.
3. "I would," her friend replied, "but I already spend all of my spare time as a volunteer at the hospital."
4. "Perhaps the most valuable result of all education," said Thomas Huxley, "is the ability to make yourself do the thing you have to do, when it ought to be done, whether you like it or not."
5.
6. "Sometimes when fate kicks us and we finally land and look around, we find we have been kicked upstairs," said Carl Sandburg.
7. "Education does not mean teaching people to know what they do not know," said John Ruskin. "It means teaching them to behave as they do not behave."
8. "Let's go to McDonald's," she said.
9. "Do you want to go now or after the movie?" he asked.
10. "Why not both times?" she said.

EXERCISE 5

1. The doctor asked, "Can you read that chart in the corner?"
2. "Touchdown!" shouted the crowd.
3. "Is this the street that Franklin Lacy lives on?" the woman asked.
4. "No," the boy replied, "he lives on the next street."
5. He said, "I'd go if I could."
6.

7. "I can't go," he said. "I have to work."
8. "A friend is a person with whom I may be sincere. Before him I may think aloud," wrote Ralph Waldo Emerson.
9. Adlai Stevenson said, "With all its sham, drudgery, and broken dreams, it is still a beautiful world."
10. Napoleon once remarked, "The only conquests which are permanent, and leave no regrets, are our conquests over ourselves."

EXERCISE 6

1. On observing the great number of civic statues, Cato, the Roman, remarked, "I would rather people would ask why there is not a statue of Cato, than why there is."
2. "Nobody can carry three watermelons under one arm," says a Spanish proverb.
3. "The taller the bamboo grows the lower it bends," says a Japanese proverb.
4.
5.
6. "That's odd," my father said.
7. "We'll do our best to get the programs printed in time," the printer said, "but we can't promise."
8. "If we knew more," said Herbert Spencer, "we would be more modest."
9. "The Cathedral of St. John the Divine in New York City is one of the two largest cathedrals in the world," said our guide.
10. Have you read "The Telltale Heart" or any other stories by Edgar Allan Poe?

EXERCISE 7

1. Do you read *Newsweek?*
2. I have been reading *Comfortable Words,* a book about word origins by Bergan Evans.
3. "All my spare time," she said, "is spent in doing volunteer work at the YWCA."
4. "Have you been back to the old school since we graduated?" he asked.
5. "I've been back once," she replied, "but nothing's the same."
6. "You may have until Monday," the instructor said, "to finish the assignment."
7. "The best way out is always through," said Robert Frost.
8. Henry David Thoreau said, "The cost of a thing is the amount of what I call life which is required to be exchanged for it immediately or in the long run."
9.
10. Have you read *Future Shock* by Alvin Toffler?

EXERCISE 8

1. "The Secret Life of Walter Mitty" is James Thurber's most popular short story.
2. "The Catbird Seat" is another popular story by Thurber.
3. "Whatever you have you must either use or lose," said Henry Ford.
4.
5. "The hottest places in Hell," said Dante, "are reserved for those who in a period of moral crisis maintain their neutrality."
6. We went to see *The Wild Duck*, one of Ibsen's plays that is not presented very often.
7. "At the end," said Richard E. Byrd, "only two things really matter to a man, regardless of who he is; and they are the affection and understanding of his family."
8. "The sword is always conquered by the spirit," is one of Napoleon's most famous sayings.
9. Benjamin Franklin said, "Dost thou love life? Then do not squander time, for that is the stuff life is made of."
10. "The man who does not do more work than he's paid for," said Abraham Lincoln, "isn't worth what he gets."

EXERCISE 9

1. An art critic once said, "There are three kinds of people in the world: those who can't stand Picasso, those who can't stand Raphael, and those who've never heard of either of them."
2.
3.
4. "Some people can stay longer in an hour than others can in a week," said William Dean Howells.
5. After her weekend visitors left, she remarked, "Guests always bring pleasure—if not in the coming, then in the going."
6. Henry David Thoreau, when asked if he had traveled much, replied, "I have traveled widely in Concord."
7. Sir James Jeans wrote, "There are at least as many stars as grains of sand upon all the seashores of the earth."
8.
9. "Man's mind stretched to a new idea never goes back to its original dimensions," said Oliver Wendell Holmes.
10. "Are you coming," she asked, "or shall I go on?"

EXERCISE 10

1. "I can't always recognize fragments," he said. "How can I be sure of them?"
2. "A fragment isn't finished," she said. "It leaves you up in the air. You are waiting for something more."
3. "I guess I just need a lot more practice in picking out fragments," he said.

4. Pablo Casals, the great cellist, spent hours on a single phrase. He said, "People say I play as easily as a bird sings. If they only knew how much effort their bird has put into his song."

5. "Why aren't you writing your essay?" I asked.

6. "Because I can't think of a thesis statement," she replied.

7. "Try some free writing," I suggested, "and you may get an idea."

8. Harry Overstreet, writing in his book *The Mature Mind,* says, "To hate and to fear is to be psychologically ill."

9.

10. In the novel *Fathers and Sons* by Turgenev, the main character says that the chief thing is to be able to devote yourself.

Capital Letters (p. 180)

EXERCISE 1

1. Mother
2.
3. Spain
4. English
5. South, *Gone with the Wind*

6.
7.
8. Coach
9.
10. Middle West

EXERCISE 2

1. "In Flanders Fields"
2.
3. Spanish
4. *Time, Ebony*
5.

6. Dad
7. Quincy Rink
8.
9. Missouri River
10. Britain, France

EXERCISE 3

1. Labor Day
2.
3. Rotary Club
4. African
5.

6. Fourth of July
7.
8. United Kingdom
9. Mom
10. West

EXERCISE 4

1.
2. Belmont Avenue
3.
4. Park Avenue
5. English

6. Russian
7. East
8.
9. Coal Company
10. *Silent Spring*

EXERCISE 5

1. Latin America
2. Mexico, Central, South America
3.
4. University of Calcutta, India
5. College

6. "Stopping by Woods on a Snowy Evening"
7.
8. Valentine's Day
9. Spanish, English
10. Professor, French

EXERCISE 6

1. Aquarium, Grant Park
2. Main Street, Saturday
3. Times Square, New Year's Eve
4. A, A
5.

6.
7. Uncle
8. Canal, River
9. Stanford University
10. Middle West, East

EXERCISE 7

1. *How to Win Friends and Influence People*
2. Sis
3. Arabic, English
4. Southern California, San Gabriel Mountains, San Fernando Valley
5. West Coast, Yukon
6.
7. "Tougher Meat Laws Needed in Ontario"
8. You've
9. Art 103, History 200
10. University

EXERCISE 8

1. Yosemite National Park
2. Mom
3. Gumbart Building
4.
5. Simpkins Hall, Browne Hall
6. *Games People Play*
7. Williston, North Dakota
8. Waterville High School, Kansas
9. *The Cherry Orchard*
10. *Huckleberry Finn*

EXERCISE 9

1. Rockies, West Coast
2. Middle West
3. Sunday
4. the East
5. Dad, Mother
6. Thursday, Women's Club
7. Kings Canyon National Park
8. Sis
9. Galesburg High School
10. American, Emancipation Proclamation

EXERCISE 10

1. Vietnam War
2.
3. Aunt
4. History 201, Math 200, English 101, Psychology 100.
5. English
6. What's
7.
8. Mother, Father, Thanksgiving
9.
10. Dr.

Review of Punctuation and Capital Letters (p. 184)

EXERCISE 1

1. You'll find them where you left them, Son.
2. Psychology, the class I like best, comes at eight; history comes at four.
3. I sent the letter to 413 Roosevelt Road, Chicago, but it came back unopened.
4. Emily Dickinson's terse, brittle style in poetry has won her a large audience.
5. I sent my application to the University of California, Berkeley, California.
6. When Max came up to visit me, we went to see Sandra, who is in the hospital.
7. We tried to be fair to him; moreover we encouraged him to resign before his actions became known.
8. Lee Fraser, the dean of our college, is an understanding person.
9. "Yes, I'll do it for you," she said. "When shall I begin?"
10. His knapsack contained the following items: food, matches, and a sleeping bag.

EXERCISE 2

1. Severton Hotel, the old abandoned hotel on the south side of town, burned last year.
2. He was hurt on April 20, 1976, and he's been in the St. Francis Hospital ever since.
3. I'm glad it's snowing; now we can go skiing tomorrow.
4. Although I have not read *Ghosts,* I have read a number of other plays by Ibsen.
5. Success is getting what you want; happiness is wanting what you get.
6.
7. "The trouble with the average family," said Bill Vaughan, "is it has too much month left over at the end of the money."
8. "Life," said Samuel Butler, "is like playing a violin solo in public and learning the instrument as one goes on."
9. The lecturer spoke for over an hour, but the audience did not grow restless.
10. Yes, I suppose I am partial; nevertheless I have tried to be fair.

EXERCISE 3

1. My writing has improved greatly, but I still have a way to go.
2. Since I have learned to write a thesis statement with supporting reasons, I now find essay writing much easier.
3. Some people are affected by gloomy weather; it has no effect on me.
4. I have three reasons for not going: money, time, and lack of interest.
5. I decided, moreover, to cancel my subscription.

6. A little old lady from Boston refused to travel, saying, "Why should I travel? I'm here already."
7. Leal stated, however, that the committee was working on the problem.
8. Lend me a pencil, Jeannette.
9. Two years later Milton left Cambridge and went to Horton, a little village west of London.
10. Coming out of the Capitol, the senator said, "You save a billion here and a billion there, and it soon mounts up."

EXERCISE 4

1. No, he didn't come; we'll miss him.
2. An Arabian proverb says, "I had no shoes and complained until I met a man who had no feet."
3. You should see Berta's room, Mother; it's decorated in tan, blue, and cerise.
4. Virgil Folsom, my old school friend, has gone to the University of New Hampshire to study.
5. "What's wrong?" she asked.
6. He cried, "Give me liberty or give me death."
7. Don't be frightened, Buddy.
8. The following men are on the affirmative side: Harris, Wilson, and Boyer.
9. In 1973 man made his deepest penetration into the earth—11,391 feet—in Transvaal, South Africa.
10. "Are you going to town, or are you going to study?" she asked.

EXERCISE 5

1. Gandhi said, "Monotony is the law of nature. Look at the monotonous manner in which the sun rises. The monotony of necessary occupations is exhilarating and life-giving."
2. Can the story be true, then, that we read in the paper?
3. *The Christian Science Monitor* and *The Wall Street Journal* are excellent newspapers.
4. She spoke, furthermore, of our neglect of our duties.
5. I didn't study; I went to a party instead.
6. Then I called on John Miller, the local tailor.
7. Her attitude, it seems to me, is antagonistic.
8. I knew just what to say, for I had been told what she would ask.
9.
10. The Taj Mahal, which is in Agra, is often called the most beautiful building in the world.

EXERCISE 6

1. The gutters were full of water; it was difficult to cross the street.
2. Figure skating, which I am just learning, takes hours of practice.
3.

4. "Full speed ahead," ordered the captain.
5. As we put the horses in their stalls, we could hear my father calling us.
6.
7. In the shop we found native handicraft: drums, grass skirts, and tapa cloth.
8. Her house in Georgetown, where I visited every summer, was one place I always felt I could return to.
9. Well, what makes you think that?
10. All of these experiences had given Wordsworth a feeling of mingled appreciation, reverence, and love for the earth.

EXERCISE 7

1. "Kenneth," she said, "your help has made all the difference."
2. He tried to improve his vocabulary by looking up new words, by keeping word lists, and by using the words in his conversation.
3. There is much inferior paint on the market, but most consumer dissatisfaction arises from bad application.
4. William Butler Yeats, who won the Nobel Prize in literature in 1923, was an Irish poet.
5. There is much more to the story, but I haven't time to tell you now.
6. The child fought, bit, kicked, and screamed, but his mother remained calm.
7. When I was in high school, I memorized Robert Frost's poem "The Road Not Taken."
8. I've never had any experience, but I think I could handle the job.
9. Our clock had stopped; we almost missed the train.
10. Gretchen then moved to Houghton, Michigan, where she played in the Keweenaw Symphony.

EXERCISE 8

1. As soon as the snow was gone, we spaded the ground and planted our seeds.
2.
3. He wrote a noble, generous letter to his old friend.
4. The highest speed ever achieved on land is 650 mph at Bonneville Salt Flats, Utah, on October 23, 1970.
5. The embittered, egotistical woman lived the life of a hermit.
6. Looking at television, playing baseball, and reading comics are my favorite pastimes.
7. Much could be done; much has been done.
8. One of the girls got an *A;* the rest got *C*'s.
9. We followed the trail to the clearing; then we turned south.
10. You know, Mom, ten dollars doesn't go far these days.

EXERCISE 9

1. Wheat, corn, and barley are widely grown in the United States.
2. We had finished our chores, and we thought we deserved a break.
3. Hey! Wait a minute! I need that book.
4. I need to do the following things: improve my spelling, get rid of wordiness, and use more specific details in my essays.
5. I must not, however, neglect my other courses.
6. Allison, one of the best students in the senior class, has the lead in the play.
7. My mother, who is not a writer herself, is still a good critic.
8. Have you seen *The Glass Menagerie* by Tennessee Williams?
9. Ursula, a young eighty-four-year-old, shares with me her enjoyment of literature and living.
10. The sign in the dentist's office read, "Support your dentist. Eat candy."

EXERCISE 10

1. Dan, one of my best friends, is entering the university in the fall.
2. John D. Rockefeller, Jr., said that every right implies a responsibility, every opportunity an obligation, every possession a duty.
3. The Bastille fell on July 14, 1789.
4. The three main forms of business organization are proprietorship, partnership, and corporation.
5. Lester is an unusually cooperative, intelligent, and helpful person.
6. Skiing, skating, and tobogganing were their chief winter sports.
7. Do you read *Time* or *Newsweek?*
8. I've changed my mind; I'm not going.
9. Those were good suggestions, Duane.
10. Helen, who uses rare critical judgment in her typing, does her work not only well but willingly.

Summary of "The Right to Die" (p. 197)

When I knew that my newborn son suffered from mongolism, I decided, though with feelings of guilt, to put him in a sanitarium where he would be well cared for but where his life would not be prolonged artificially. Thus my wife and I would be free to devote ourselves to our normal son. I believe it is time we had a humane law permitting euthanasia. I do not know how it should be practiced, but I do know that there are thousands of children on this earth whose lives are meaningless to themselves and an agony to their parents.

I have found out if you lag you end up in a drag.

I believe if you don't strive for what you what it will not come to you, you must go out and get yours. Get it! It's There.

Leon Walker

Your Spelling List

advice
advise

Angle dust

This drug is: ~~Bad~~ for Everybody
"   "   should be used for
its true purpose AND THATS All.